"*An Unfinished Council* is a hopeful book by one of the church's foremost interpreters of Vatican II. Avoiding simplistic sound-bites and worn-out clichés, Gaillardetz offers a fresh account of the council, ready for the new life breathed into the church by Pope Francis. This is a mature and magnanimous vision that, like Francis, reminds us that we all have a role to play in the ongoing reform and renewal of the church. Everyone—from the beginning undergraduate to the seasoned pastor—can learn something from Gaillardetz."

 —Edward P. Hahnenberg, PhD
  Author of *Theology for Ministry: An Introduction for Lay Ministers*

"Coming from one of the eminent ecclesiologists in the Catholic Church today, this book is a substantial contribution to the literature on Vatican II and, indeed, takes it on a new trajectory. Using his image of 'seven pillars,' Gaillardetz succinctly captures the structure of a Vatican II church. With his perceptive analysis of the council's implicit vision of 'non-competitive' ecclesial relationships in a church that is 'magnanimous' and 'humble,' Gaillardetz has given us a compelling account of the work that still needs to be done, if the vision of Vatican II is to be realized. For anyone wanting keen insight into the reform agenda of the council, and its implications for today, *An Unfinished Council* provides an inspiring guide."

 —Ormond Rush
  Australian Catholic University

"In *An Unfinished Council*, Richard R. Gaillardetz extends a compelling invitation to the Roman Catholic Church to take the next steps in its faithful pilgrimage. Beginning with an exploration of the theological principles and historical realities operative before, during, and after Vatican II, Gaillardetz proceeds to highlight humility and magnanimity as essential ecclesial virtues that develop authentic self-understanding and create collaboration rather than competition. By examining Pope Francis's reception of Vatican II, Gaillardetz encourages his readers to be architects of the church's communion and mission who engage the periphery through listening and subsidiarity. *An Unfinished Council* is an accessible, insightful, and timely call for the church to engage today in ongoing reform through critical reception of the past and with hope for the future."

 —Amanda C. Osheim
  Assistant Professor of Practical Theology
  Loras College

D1590001

"Gaillardetz is a master builder at the site of a new church under construction. Here he probes and assesses with precision the lingering remnants of obsolete pre–Vatican II church structures and practices. And with inspiring resolve and creativity he contributes to a synthetic interpretation of Vatican II's ecclesiological achievement. His blueprint accentuates the power of the Spirit in confronting the misuse of hierarchic power, while creating a new noncompetitive ordering of relationships in the church, motivated by magnanimity and humility."

—Bradford Hinze
Fordham University

"*An Unfinished Council* is an important synthesis of the meaning of Vatican II for the contemporary church, especially for the broad ideological spectrum of Catholic political engagement. It demonstrates how to resist the polarizing ideological divides facing Catholicism in America today."

—Massimo Faggioli
Director, Institute for Catholicism and Citizenship
University of St. Thomas

"The Second Vatican Council awakened Catholic consciousness to the time-conditioned nature of the church as a human community led through history toward its final fulfillment by the dynamic of God's Spirit. As such, it will always be an unfinished building project. Building on this metaphor, Richard R. Gaillardetz invites us to consider the unfinished business of receiving the council's central insights, developing a synthetic reading of its teaching apt to inform the pastoral life and missional witness of Catholics in today's world. He argues convincingly that Pope Francis presents Catholics with a fuller integration of Vatican II's enduring significance for our time, especially in his holistic vision of the church as a community of missionary disciples, confidently assuming responsibility for humble self-examination, ongoing renewal and reform, dialogical engagement within the church and with others, proclaiming the mercy and justice of God. Superbly written, a balanced, creative, and insightful reading of the challenges and opportunities facing contemporary Catholicism."

—Catherine E. Clifford
Professor of Systematic and Historical Theology
Saint Paul University, Ottawa

An Unfinished Council

Vatican II, Pope Francis, and the Renewal of Catholicism

Richard R. Gaillardetz

A Michael Glazier Book

LITURGICAL PRESS

Collegeville, Minnesota

www.litpress.org

A Michael Glazier Book published by Liturgical Press

Cover design by Jodi Hendrickson. Cover image © Thinkstock.

Unless otherwise indicated, excerpts from documents of the Second Vatican Council are from *Vatican Council II: Constitutions, Decrees, Declarations; The Basic Sixteen Documents*, edited by Austin Flannery, OP, © 1996. Used with permission of Liturgical Press, Collegeville, Minnesota.

Scripture texts in this work are taken from the *New Revised Standard Version Bible*, © 1989, Division of Christian Education of the National Council of the Churches of Christ in the United States of America. Used by permission. All rights reserved.

© 2015 by Order of Saint Benedict, Collegeville, Minnesota. All rights reserved. No part of this book may be reproduced in any form, by print, microfilm, microfiche, mechanical recording, photocopying, translation, or by any other means, known or yet unknown, for any purpose except brief quotations in reviews, without the previous written permission of Liturgical Press, Saint John's Abbey, PO Box 7500, Collegeville, Minnesota 56321-7500. Printed in the United States of America.

1   2   3   4   5   6   7   8   9

Library of Congress Cataloging-in-Publication Data

Gaillardetz, Richard R., 1958–
    An unfinished council : Vatican II, Pope Francis, and the renewal of Catholicism / Richard R. Gaillardetz.
        pages   cm
    "A Michael Glazier Book."
    ISBN 978-0-8146-8309-5 — ISBN 978-0-8146-8334-7 (ebook)
    1. Vatican Council (2nd : 1962–1965 : Basilica di San Pietro in Vaticano)   2. Catholic Church—History—1965–   3. Catholic Church—Doctrines.   4. Francis, Pope, 1936– —Influence.   5. Church renewal—Catholic Church.   I. Title.

BX8301962 .G283 2015
262'.52—dc23   2015006953

To Robert Rivers, CSP,
who first introduced me to the Second Vatican Council

Contents

Preface   ix

Chapter 1: The Council in Context: Responding to the
            Hierocratic Form of the Church   1

Chapter 2: The Council That Almost Failed   29

Chapter 3: Toward a New Ecclesial Form: The Pillars
            of Vatican II's Ecclesial Vision   49

Chapter 4: Vatican II and the Humility of the Church   73

Chapter 5: A Noncompetitive Theology of the Church   91

Chapter 6: Pope Francis and the Reception of Vatican II   115

Chapter 7: From a Pastoral Council to a Pastoral Renewal   137

Bibliography   159

Index   167

Preface

The Second Vatican Council was an event of unparalleled significance in the history of modern Catholicism. One has to go back to the Protestant Reformation to find an event that matches Vatican II's impact on Roman Catholicism. In December 2015 the Catholic Church celebrates the fiftieth anniversary of the close of that groundbreaking council. Yet for all its historic importance, many millennial Catholics have greeted the council's anniversary with one big ecclesial yawn. Understandably, young Catholics mostly take for granted the council's most important achievements because those achievements constitute, in many ways, the only church reality they have known. Older Catholics are generally more aware of the changes introduced at the council. Yet even as they acknowledge conciliar contributions like the liturgical reform, a more prominent role for the laity and a more positive spirit of dialogue with other Christian traditions and world religions, they often fail to grasp the emerging theological vision that informed those developments.

Among various Catholic elites—clergy, lay ministers, church activists, theologians, and church commentators—the celebration of this anniversary has been more complex. Some have cautiously acknowledged the council's contributions but not without considerable handwringing regarding its proper interpretation. They worry that there has been insufficient appreciation for the substantial continuity between the council and what came before. They acknowledge valid theological developments but insist that the council effected no change at the level of church doctrine. For such Catholics, the council's primary contribution was limited to its change in pastoral tone and a circumscribed empowerment of the laity, in the secular order. Still many others, including a good number old enough to appreciate the council's importance, struggle between two impulses: gratitude for the gift of the council and discouragement at the extent to which important conciliar teachings have yet to be fully implemented. They are exasperated, in short, with the council's failed promise. If their disappointment is warranted, and to some extent I believe it is, where does one locate the origins of that failure?

To begin with, the council suffered the misfortune of having been convened right as the Western world underwent a cultural cataclysm of sorts in the 1960s and 1970s. Widespread social unrest brought about by the Cuban missile crisis, unruly student protests, the civil rights movement, the sexual revolution, the assassination of one American president, the scandal-induced resignation of another, and, at least in the United States, a wildly unpopular war—all contributed to a cultural climate that made it difficult to distinguish legitimate calls for church reform from the larger *zeitgeist* of social unrest.

In hindsight, there may also have been a certain naïveté regarding the challenges the church faced in producing a structural implementation of the council's reformist vision. For example, the revised 1984 *Code of Canon Law* represented a major effort to give juridical form to the council's teaching. Yet in spite of the revised code's slavish quotation of the council documents, it too often failed to grasp the council's overarching theological vision. Hervé Legrand writes:

> *Vatican II paid scant attention to the canonical dimension of the reforms it sought to introduce.* Of all the Council documents, only the Constitution on the Liturgy concerned itself with guaranteeing its enactment, setting out forty-nine(!) normative prescriptions. After this, *Christus Dominus* was virtually the only document to use this method, though it set out wishes rather than norms.[1]

The task of postconciliar reform was handed over to the Roman Curia for implementation. In the area of the liturgy, a bold experiment at postconciliar reform was undertaken with the creation of the Consilium, a special commission of bishops and liturgical experts. This remarkable commission, headed by Cardinal Giacomo Lercaro of Bologna and driven by the indefatigable liturgical scholar Anni-

[1] Hervé Legrand, "Forty Years Later: What Has Become of the Ecclesiological Reforms Envisaged by Vatican II?," in *Concilium: Vatican II: A Forgotten Future*, ed. Alberto Melloni and Christoph Theobald, no. 4 (2005): 57–72, at 57; emphasis in original.

bale Bugnini, undertook the monumental task of revising the entire corpus of liturgical books and rituals, culminating in the Missal of Pope Paul VI. The commission lasted from 1964 to 1969; its unusual independence from the Curia and its reputation for collaboration and a high level of liturgical scholarship allowed it to provide a far-reaching implementation of the council's liturgical vision. Yet there were obvious limits to its work, given its chronological proximity to the council. In 1969 its mission was taken over by the Congregation of Divine Worship, and while that congregation ably continued the liturgical reform over the next five years, it inevitably exerted what Piero Marini referred to as a "curialization" of the liturgical reform.[2] This became even more pronounced some six years later when, in 1975, the Congregation for Divine Worship and the Congregation for the Discipline of the Sacraments were combined into one curial office. Crimped postconciliar implementation was even more pronounced in other areas. The curialization of reform basically meant asking a bureaucracy with a native inclination to preserve the *status quo* to take responsibility for reforming itself!

Yet another difficulty, and the one that will occupy most of our attention in this volume, concerns the ongoing need for more synthetic theological interpretations of the council's teaching and enduring significance. The council provided no unified and comprehensive ecclesiology. Instead, what we find in the council documents are important theological and pastoral trajectories for development across a range of issues. Given how councils work, this is understandable, but the consequence was that it has been too easy to isolate particular council teachings in a way that minimizes the broader conciliar impulse for meaningful church reform. So, for example, it has been too easy to highlight the council's teaching on the laity but without linking it to the council's teaching on the capacity of all the baptized to actively appropriate God's Word in their lives (the council's teaching on the *sensus fidei*). What has too often resulted is a celebration

---

[2] Piero Marini, *A Challenging Reform: Realizing the Vision of the Liturgical Renewal* (Collegeville, MN: Liturgical Press, 2007), 153. See also Rita Ferrone, *Liturgy*: Sacrosanctum Concilium, Rediscovering Vatican II Series (New York: Paulist Press, 2007), 61.

of lay volunteerism that still excludes the laity from contributing substantively to church decision making.

Over the past five decades, we have seen the publication of many helpful commentaries on the conciliar texts. Countless other books and articles have engaged in a focused exegesis of controverted passages and formulations found in the conciliar texts. The distinguished French Canadian expert in the study of Vatican II, Gilles Routhier, notes both the contributions and limits of these more focused studies:

> Necessary and legitimate though this analytic method is, it tends, if it is not accompanied by a more synthetic method, to dismember the conciliar corpus by reducing it to so many instructions on specific questions. It tends to concentrate on particular, isolated pronouncements, thereby preventing a grasp of Vatican II as a coherent whole or a unified ensemble and reducing it to an aggregate of specific teachings. In effect, it is possible to gloss on and to comment *ad infinitum* on the teachings of the council—on *subsistit in*, for example, or the hierarchy of truths—without ever arriving at a grasp of the council's central intuitions that should still be nourishing us today.[3]

Any synthetic study of the council must carefully attend to the council texts, read in the light of their textual history, their intra/intertextual contexts, and their postconciliar reception.[4] But a synthetic study will also, as Routhier notes, consider the distinctive theological method that the council employed, its characteristic way of addressing issues and framing questions that needed to be explored. It will look for seminal ideas, larger patterns, and architectonic structures that informed the council's deliberations.[5]

This volume marks my own preliminary contribution to a more synthetic interpretation of the council. I do not claim to offer an exhaustive and comprehensive interpretation of the council's teaching; such a project, I suspect, is no longer within the capacity of a

---

[3] Gilles Routhier, "Vatican II: Relevance and Future," *Theological Studies* 74 (September 2013): 537–54, at 540.

[4] For a fruitful development of this threefold hermeneutical strategy see Ormond Rush, *Still Interpreting Vatican II: Some Hermeneutical Principles* (New York: Paulist Press, 2004).

[5] Routhier, "Vatican II: Relevance and Future," 541.

single theologian. Some of what the council taught will have to be given only cursory consideration here. Nevertheless, my goal in this volume is to contribute to the theological task of drawing together the council's many contributions into a more coherent theological vision of the church, one capable of underwriting a comprehensive program of ecclesial reform and renewal.

This project will be structured around a useful metaphor for the council once offered by the distinguished German theologian Hermann Pottmeyer. At the conclusion of a volume he wrote on the papacy, Pottmeyer referred to Vatican II as "an unfinished building site," an ecclesiological project still waiting completion.[6] He recalled the rebuilding of St. Peter's Basilica in the sixteenth century. The original basilica had been built during the Constantinian era and was, by the sixteenth century, rather dilapidated. Over much of the sixteenth century, a series of popes sponsored the design and construction of a new basilica, one more adequate to the needs of the church. The work began on the construction of a new basilica, however, even as portions of the older Constantinian basilica were left standing. The remains of the older basilica would not be completely removed until almost a century after the new building project had begun. Pottmeyer saw in this sixteenth-century tableau an extended metaphor for the work of the council. It too was responding to an outdated ecclesial form and its work represented the partial construction of an alternative ecclesial form more adequate to the needs of the time. Following Pottmeyer's intuition, I contend that Vatican II can be imagined as an ecclesiological building project concerned with constructing a new "basilica," that is, a renewed vision for the church. Yet this project was undertaken in the shadow of a still imposing but largely antiquated ecclesial "structure."

The metaphor helps explain the title of this volume, *An Unfinished Council: Vatican II, Pope Francis, and the Renewal of Catholicism*. It should go without saying that I go beyond Pottmeyer's more modest employment of the metaphor and any failures that accompany this effort should be placed at my feet and not his. The building metaphor is helpful, in my view, because it brings into relief the necessary

---

[6] Hermann J. Pottmeyer, *Towards a Papacy in Communion: Perspectives from Vatican Councils I & II* (New York: Crossroad, 1998), 110.

historical contextualization of the council. It acknowledges that the pope's decision to call the council was born out of a sober assessment of the state of the Catholic Church at that time. The pope and many other church leaders and theologians had come to feel the burdensome strain of striving to fulfill the church's mission within a theological, sacramental, and pastoral form that in many instances was no longer adequate to the demands of that mission. At the same time, the metaphor allows us to appreciate the extent to which the council's response represented the beginning of a new theological, sacramental, and pastoral form (the beginnings of the new "basilica"), albeit a form that could not be completed. According to Pottmeyer, the council was able to establish the "pillars" for a new structure but could not provide a "dome" that would bring those pillars into an architectural unity. Hence Vatican II has remained an unfinished project.

We must be careful to recognize the limits and dangers that go with employing extended metaphors of this kind. First of all, the building metaphor is inherently static, whereas the reality it wishes to illuminate, the Catholic Church and its great tradition, is a living, dynamic reality. Second, the metaphor foregrounds the inadequacies of the preconciliar "form" of the Catholic Church and the council's bold call for reform and renewal. As a consequence, it privileges the novelty of the council, somewhat at the expense of the council's continuity with past ecclesial forms. By emphasizing change over continuity, the metaphor is at least susceptible to the criticism of Pope Benedict XVI, who famously counterposed two different ways of interpreting Vatican II.[7] First, he criticized the emergence of a "hermeneutics of discontinuity and rupture" that posited a radical discontinuity between Vatican II and the earlier Catholic tradition. He then proposed, not a hermeneutics of continuity, as one might expect, but a "hermeneutics of reform," an interpretive strategy that acknowledges in the council's teaching a "novelty in continuity." He recognized that there was genuine novelty in the council's teaching, but a novelty that deepened fidelity with the great tradition of the church.

---

[7] He offered this hermeneutical analysis in a pre-Christmas address given on December 22, 2005. The text can be found online at: http://www.vatican .va/holy_father/benedict_xvi/speeches/2005/december/documents/hf_ben_xvi _spe_20051222_roman-curia_en.html.

The pope was surely right to insist that a formal and comprehensive rendering of the council's relationship to the great tradition must seek a balanced consideration of elements of both continuity and change.[8] The council's teaching did far more than merely salvage select elements from an antiquated ecclesial form; it drew considerably from a rich two thousand-year heritage, but often bringing into the foreground of church reflection elements from that heritage that had been neglected or minimized in the older form.

As Pope John XXIII himself noted in his opening address at the council, however, there was really no need to call for an ecumenical council if such a council were to do no more than repeat what has always been taught. Pope John convoked Vatican II in order to address pressing challenges in both the church and the world. It was in this sense that Vatican II was to be a "pastoral" council. The council bishops made clear choices to attend to certain questions and issues at the expense of others. The council deliberations constituted a practical assessment of the state of the church at that time and a determination to bring about a necessary reform and renewal. If, then, our efforts at a constructive and synthetic interpretation of the council are to be in keeping with the pastoral orientation of the council itself, a measured emphasis on change over continuity may be warranted. Granting these limits, I contend that the building metaphor, if used judiciously, remains useful as a way of illuminating the fundamental orientation and genuine contributions of the council.

Chapter 1 begins with a brief consideration of the key features of the ancient "basilica," what I will refer to as the preconciliar, "hierocratic" form of the church. It is this form, the result of centuries of development, which shaped Catholic identity for good and for ill in the early twentieth century. The dramatic advance of biblical and historical studies that flourished in the nineteenth and early twentieth centuries allowed Catholics to appreciate that this hierocratic form was just that, a form and not *the* form of the church. The emerging historical consciousness that permeated the intellectual life of Roman Catholicism during that period made possible a thoroughgoing assessment and critique of the hierocratic form.

---

[8] An apt example of such a project would be Cardinal Walter Kasper's *The Catholic Church: Nature, Reality, and Mission* (New York: Bloomsbury, 2015).

Chapter 2 will consider the council as an "event" that itself manifested a new way of being church.[9] The story of the council is, in a sense, the story of the church in microcosm. It is the story of the church in the process of what Joseph Komonchak referred to as the church's "self-constitution."[10] The story of the council is, then, the story of the church seeking a renewed fidelity to the great tradition precisely by being church in a new way. Chapter 3 follows upon this consideration of the council as event by returning to the building metaphor to present a "wide-angle lens" view of the council's principal contributions toward a new ecclesial self-understanding. Here we will encounter a number of important conciliar developments that lacked, however, a unifying theological narrative.

Chapters 4 and 5 will begin the project of constructing a synthetic interpretation of the council's ecclesiological achievement. Chapter 4 considers council teaching with regard to the fundamental orientation of the church, an orientation governed by the ecclesial virtue of humility. Chapter 5 offers a complementary reading of council teaching, but now attending to ecclesial dynamics, that is, an exploration of how various components or spheres of ecclesial life are called to interact. If the organizing principle of chapter 4 was the virtue of humility, the organizing principle of chapter 5 is the council's recovery of pneumatology, a theology of the Holy Spirit that enables a shift from a competitive to a noncompetitive account of ecclesial dynamics. Chapter 6 considers the extent to which the pontificate of Pope Francis is offering a fresh reception of the teaching of the council that represents, in its own way, yet another effort at a more

---

[9] Joseph Komonchak and John O'Malley have each, in distinct ways, emphasized the way in which Vatican II must be appreciated, not only for the authoritative teaching evident in the sixteen documents it promulgated, but also as an ecclesial "event" that constituted a decisive "rupture" with the ordinary course of church life. See Joseph Komonchak, "Vatican II as 'Event,'" Fourth Annual De Lubac Lecture, February 11, 1999 (privately published by the Department of Theological Studies and the Office of University Mission and Ministry, St. Louis University, St. Louis, 1999); John W. O'Malley, "Vatican II: Did Anything Happen?," *Theological Studies* 67 (2006): 3–33.

[10] Joseph Komonchak, "The Significance of Vatican II for Ecclesiology," in *The Gift of the Church: A Textbook on Ecclesiology*, ed. Peter Phan (Collegeville, MN: Liturgical Press, A Michael Glazier Book, 2000), 70.

synthetic interpretation of the council's teaching. In conclusion, chapter 7 offers some reflections on the possible direction of a program for reform and renewal consonant with the council's implicit ecclesiological vision.

This volume includes both newly developed material and a thorough reworking of material from essays of mine that originally appeared elsewhere. These include: "Conversation Starters: Dialogue and Deliberation during Vatican II," *America* (February 13, 2012): 14–18; "We Have the Pillars, but the Building Is Still Unfinished," in *A Church Reborn: Second Vatican Council, 1962–1965*, special edition of the *National Catholic Reporter* (October 11, 2012): 48–50; "Engaging Magisterial Activism Today," *Horizons* 39, no. 2 (2012): 230–51; "Building on Vatican II: Setting the Agenda for the Church of the 21st Century," *Theoforum* 44 (2013): 67–90; "Vatican II's Noncompetitive Theology of the Church," *Louvain Studies* 37 (2013): 3–27; "The 'Francis Moment': A New Kairos for Catholic Ecclesiology," *CTSA Proceedings* 69 (2014): 63–80; "Vatican II and the Humility of the Church," in *The Legacy of Vatican II*, edited by Massimo Faggioli and Andrea Vicini (New York: Paulist Press, 2015); "Power and Authority in the Church: Emerging Issues," in *A Church with Open Doors: Catholic Ecclesiology for the Third Millennium*, edited by Richard R. Gaillardetz and Edward P. Hahnenberg (Collegeville, MN: Liturgical Press, 2015).

I am grateful for the ongoing support of Boston College and for my many marvelous colleagues and graduate students in our theology department, including especially my graduate assistant Kevin Brown who assisted in copyediting this manuscript. I want to thank Peter Dwyer and Hans Christoffersen at Liturgical Press for their friendship and continued encouragement. I owe a special debt of gratitude to two good friends and colleagues, James Bacik and Catherine Clifford, for their willingness to comment on early versions of this manuscript.

My "true companion," Diana, has walked with me for almost three decades and her support has sustained me in ways too deep and textured to be adequately expressed in these brief acknowledgments. Our four sons (Greg, Brian, David, and Andrew) are now adults; they remain a source of boundless pride. The joy they give me has fueled so much of my intellectual passion.

In the fall of 1977, as a nineteen-year-old sophomore attending the University of Texas, I walked into the Catholic Student Center that was adjacent to the campus. Raised in a Catholic family, I had drifted away from the practice of Catholicism during my first year of college and joined a more fundamentalist, evangelical group. I soon became disturbed, however, by the anti-intellectualism of that brand of Evangelicalism. Still dissatisfied with the tepid Catholicism of my youth, I nevertheless decided to visit the Catholic Student Center. There I met a young Paulist priest on the staff named Fr. Robert Rivers, CSP, who invited me to take a course he was teaching on modern biblical scholarship in the Catholic tradition. That course led to a series of adult education classes and numerous reading suggestions that introduced me to the capacious breadth and depth of the Catholic tradition and the beguiling promise of the Second Vatican Council. Over the next four decades, Bob has remained a dear friend, spiritual director, mentor, and golf partner. It is with immense gratitude that I dedicate these modest reflections to him.

The Council in Context

Responding to the Hierocratic Form of the Church

Enthusiastic support for the reformist program of Vatican II can lead to an unnecessary denigration of the state of Catholicism on the eve of the council. The Catholic Church before the council certainly continued to enrich the lives of many believers. The Catholic faith was still handed on in parishes and schools, and the sacraments were celebrated. Countless Catholics were led by God's grace and the practice of their faith to a life of holiness. Many Catholics had a robust sense of their own religious identity; being Catholic offered a distinctive way of being in the world. Indeed, Catholics dwelled in an enchanted world sustained by a sensual religious imagination. Sacramentals, stained-glass windows, statuary, and a plethora of devotional practices further enriched this religious imagination. The clergy were viewed as exemplars of holiness, sacramental "dispensers," and keepers of ecclesiastical order and stability. The papacy provided a strong symbol of Catholic identity and church unity.[1] Yet, as we shall see, not all was well with the church.

---

[1] For a series of helpful "snapshots" of Catholic life, at least here in the United States, in the decades before the council, see Thomas H. Groome and Michael J. Daley, eds., *Reclaiming Catholicism: Treasures Old and New* (Maryknoll, NY: Orbis Books, 2010).

In truth, the history of Catholicism has seen many different church "forms," each corresponding more or less to the historical context and pastoral challenges of a given age. Ordinary believers prayed, exercised the works of mercy, and generally practiced their faith in distinctive and characteristic ways just as church leaders exercised their particular ministries according to patterns shaped by divine revelation, cultural assumptions, and the pragmatic needs of the time. As but one example from the early church, the office of the priest had its origins in the second-century ministry of the presbyter who functioned primarily as an elder-counselor and exercised little in the way of sacramental ministry. As Christianity grew in certain urban areas, however, it was no longer possible for all the Christians of a city to gather at one place of worship under the presidency of their bishop. Satellite communities sprouted and bishops began delegating to their presbyters the responsibility of presiding at the Eucharist for these communities.

As each epoch succeeded the next, certain ecclesiastical structures, thought forms, and customary expressions of the church's self-understanding were carried forward. Some endured because they had proven to be of lasting value. Others, however, maintained a position of prominence long after the circumstances that led to their development had passed away. Catholic Christians recognize a providential character in many of these developments, but this cannot blind us to the relative contingency of particular ecclesial structures (e.g., the gradual emergence of the College of Cardinals). The church has the task, in every age, to discern which elements of the church's practice and self-understanding are enduring and providential and which are not.

Church history must not be reduced to a story of unrelieved devolution from some more ancient and presumably more pure vision of the church. Change and development are inevitable in a church that is truly alive. If we believe the Spirit continues to abide and influence the church, then we must resist imagining that only the form in which the church appeared in the first centuries represents the church willed by Christ and his Spirit. As Elisabeth Schüssler Fiorenza suggests, we should see the life and structure of the early church more as a "prototype" from which all future forms of the church must be linked, rather than as an "archetype" upon which all other ecclesial forms must be modeled.[2]

Over the course of two millennia, new theological schools emerged; religious orders were created and lay initiatives undertaken. Faith and culture interacted in particular contexts. Few Christians bothered to think in an explicitly theological way about the church, at least in the sense of engaging in formal and self-critical reflection on the nature and mission of the church. Operative ecclesiologies were simply enacted in concrete sets of communal structures and practices, some of which had long endured and others which emerged in response to changing contexts.

Over the course of the second millennium, through a succession of ecclesial epochs, a series of ecclesial forms followed one upon the other. There are any number of ways to parse these historical developments. Staf Hellemans describes three successive forms that emerged over the last five hundred years.[3] The first was the emergence of "early modern Catholicism" which, beginning in the sixteenth century, responded to the Protestant Reformation, the rise of modern science, and the beginning of the Enlightenment. The second form, which developed in the wake of the French Revolution, he describes as "ultramontane mass Catholicism." It is during this period that Catholicism emerges as a distinct counter-society and looks to the papacy as a unifying force. Papal centralization moved from rhetoric to reality as bishops are brought more fully under the ambit of papal authority. Hellemans also sees in this period an unprecedented socialization of the larger Catholic population into a particular account of Catholic identity, a socialization made possible by the employment of modern media and the widespread expansion of an ambitious Catholic educational system.

---

[2] Elisabeth Schüssler Fiorenza, *Bread Not Stone: The Challenge of Feminist Hermeneutics* (Boston: Beacon Press, 1995), 10–14.

[3] Staf Hellemans, "Tracking the New Shape of the Catholic Church in the West," in *Towards a New Catholic Church in Advanced Modernity: Transformation, Visions, Tensions*, ed. Staf Hellemans and Jozef Wissink (Zürich: Lit Verlag, 2012), 19–50.

The ecclesial form that dominated the Catholic landscape in the early twentieth century was in fact sustained by structures, ecclesial habits, and thought forms that originated in various periods of church history. In this volume, I refer to this as the "hierocratic form" of the church. I am borrowing the term from the great Dominican theologian Yves Congar, who so perceptively limned the rise of a "hierocratic ecclesiology" beginning in the eleventh century.[4] Recalling Pottmeyer's extended metaphor, this hierocratic form corresponds to the Constantinian basilica of St. Peter's. It had long served the church well but had eventually become dilapidated and was widely acknowledged as no longer adequate to the needs of the church of that time. This form was not without its strengths. It provided an unambiguous sense of distinctive Catholic identity and institutional structures that had proven extraordinarily successful in preserving the church's unity through a program of comprehensive ecclesiastical uniformity.

In this chapter I wish to outline the key features of the hierocratic form that dominated the Catholic landscape on the eve of Vatican II. Five basic "pillars" supported this hierocratic form.[5] Each pillar itself has a long history and only select moments in those histories can be noted here. These pillars are: (1) a propositional theology of divine revelation, (2) a papo-centric church leadership structure, (3) a sacral priesthood, (4) a mechanistic theology of grace and the sacraments, and (5) a confrontational attitude toward the world.

I. A Propositional Theology of Revelation

Christians do not believe that we are left here on our own to seek out some distant and inscrutable divine reality. Rather, we believe that

---

[4] Yves Congar, *L'Église de Saint Augustin à l'époque moderne* (Paris: Cerf, 1970), 224–30.

[5] Ghislain Lafont has something very similar in mind to this hierocratic form of the church in his description of what he called the "Gregorian form of the church." See Ghislain Lafont, *Imagining the Catholic Church: Structured Communion in the Spirit* (Collegeville, MN: Liturgical Press, 2000), 37–64. The first three of these "pillars" correspond loosely to Lafont's characterization of the Gregorian form; the last two represent my own expanded characterization of the hierocratic ecclesiology dominant on the eve of the council.

God wishes to disclose to us God's very self as the infinite horizon and necessary foundation for all loving and life-giving relationship. The biblical testimony recounts this event of divine communication through the mediation of God's activity on behalf of the people of Israel and the teaching of the prophets. This divine self-disclosure, early Christians believed, had achieved its unsurpassable goal in the person of Jesus of Nazareth and his decisive proclamation of the in-breaking of God's shalom into history. Divine truth was revealed in its most basic modality, not in a written text but in a person. This was the heart of a Christian theology of revelation and for centuries there was relatively little development beyond these basic convictions.

Only after some centuries, and under the influence of an over-whelmingly Platonic intellectual milieu, did a theology of revelation emerge that presented divine Truth as that which supernaturally illuminated the human intellect through faith. Under the influence of an extraordinary figure from the fifth or sixth centuries known simply as Pseudo-Dionysius, Christian Neoplatonism reconfig-ured the theology of divine revelation as a reality received from the upper spiritual realm and conveyed to the lower created realms of the cosmos. Although Pseudo-Dionysius first influenced Eastern Christianity, over the centuries his thought would be brought to the West and in the thirteenth century it began to shape Western ecclesiology. Divine revelation was presented as a reality given to the hierarchy and then handed on to the lay faithful through the agency of church officeholders. We might describe this as a kind of spiritual "trickle-down theory."[6] Divine Truth was understood as mediated in a linguistic or propositional form as a set of discrete "truths." In this view, supernatural revelation was concerned primarily with the transmission of conceptual knowledge and was conceived on the analogy of human speech. According to Ghislain Lafont, this the-ology assumed "a quasi-identity of revealed truth and the formulas expressing the truth."[7] This approach was further stimulated in the

---

[6] Richard R. Gaillardetz, *Teaching with Authority: A Theology of the Magis-terium in the Church* (Collegeville, MN: Liturgical Press, 1997), 247.

[7] Lafont, *Imagining the Catholic Church*, 39. Decades earlier, Joseph Ratzinger made a similar observation in his commentary on *Dei Verbum*. Joseph Ratzinger, "The Dogmatic Constitution on Divine Revelation," in *Commentary on the*

late Middle Ages by an excessive confidence in the capacity of syllogistic logic to generate new dogmatic propositions. Nevertheless, the church of the Middle Ages also gave ample room for wide-ranging theological debate regarding the content of divine revelation, the proper interpretation of Scripture, and the status of apparent contradictions within Scripture and tradition.[8]

Although the origins of this propositional model can be traced back to the Middle Ages, it would receive much fuller development with the rise of a brand of theology known as neoscholasticism in the hundred years or so prior to Vatican II.[9] Church officeholders, the pope and bishops who came to constitute "the magisterium," would play a distinctive and virtually exclusive role in authoritatively proposing these dogmatic propositions for belief. Since not all of the dogmatic propositions offered by the church as divinely revealed could be found in Scripture, this view led some to assert the existence of two distinct sources of revelation: Scripture and tradition.[10] In this view, while certain propositional truths were explicitly articulated in Scripture, others could only be found in tradition. This view would be reinforced by the promulgation of the Marian dogmas of the Immaculate Conception and Bodily Assumption of Mary, since both had few if any biblical warrants.

Documents of Vatican II, vol. 3, ed. Herbert Vorgrimler (New York: Crossroad, 1989), 190–91.

[8] Ian Christopher Levy, *Holy Scripture and the Quest for Authority at the End of the Middle Ages* (Notre Dame, IN: University of Notre Dame Press, 2012).

[9] Avery Dulles considers this approach to revelation as one of several different "models of revelation." In this context a given model suggests "a possible and consistent way of thinking about a certain set of problems." *Models of Revelation* (Garden City, NY: Doubleday, 1983), 31–32. Dulles refers to what I have called the propositional model as "revelation as doctrine." For his initial treatment of this model see *Models of Revelation*, 36–52.

[10] The Council of Trent had flirted with a similar (though not identical) position centuries earlier. In one of its decrees, Trent proposed that divine truths were contained "partly" in the "written books" and "partly" in unwritten traditions. The final text, however, was changed to read that truth was found "both in the written books and in unwritten traditions." The first formulation suggested that these were two distinct sources of divine truth, yet the final formulation was at least open to the interpretation that there were not different *sources* of truth at all but only different *modes of expression*.

This emphasis on revelation in the form of discrete doctrinal statements taught authoritatively by the magisterium had the merit of making the Christian faith readily intelligible; it offered a clarity regarding the content of Christian belief and provided ready answers to Catholics who needed to defend their faith against the attacks of non-Catholics. This theology, however, was also prone to reducing revelation to a set of propositional truths about God, forgetting almost entirely the ancient conviction that divine revelation has come to us first and primarily as an offer to saving communion in the person of Jesus Christ.[11]

Over the centuries, this propositional reduction of revelation gradually shaped conceptions of the role of the people of God in the handing on and reception of the faith of the church. If revelation is passively received from above through the exclusive mediation of official teaching authorities, then the reception of that revelation by the faithful will necessarily be passive and obediential, adding nothing to what has been handed down.

As we shall see, during the first session of Vatican II, the bishops were presented with a draft document on divine revelation that presupposed much of this propositional model.[12] In fact it was titled "On the Sources of Revelation." It proposed problematic understandings of the inspiration of the biblical authors and the nature of the assistance of the Holy Spirit given to the church hierarchy. In considerations of biblical authorship, for example, the draft text downplayed the human element and considered the biblical authors as little more than passive conduits of divine truth.

II. A Papo-Centric Church Leadership Structure

A robust papo-centrism represents the second "pillar" in this hierocratic form. Over the first three centuries, we can identify a quickly emerging conviction that the church of Rome, a church associated

---

[11] For examples of this model of revelation see Christian Pesch, *Praelectiones dogmaticae*, 5th ed. (Freiburg: Herder, 1915), and Reginald Garrigou-Lagrange, *De Revelatione per Ecclesiam catholicam proposita*, 4th ed. (Rome: Ferrari, 1945).

[12] Ratzinger, "Dogmatic Constitution on Divine Revelation," 155–67.

with not one but two great apostles, Sts. Peter and Paul, had a particular claim on having received the apostolic teaching and having remained faithful to that teaching. The distinctive primacy thereby attributed to the church of Rome would eventually be extended to its bishop, and by the fourth century the authority of the Bishop of Rome was further underwritten by appeals to Matthew 16 and the authority that Christ had granted to St. Peter.

Catholicism affirms the necessary role of a Petrine ministry, yet we must acknowledge the relatively marginal role of the papacy in the life of the church for much of the first millennium. For the first thousand years of Christianity, most Christians would never have seen the pope, never have read anything that he had said or written, and, indeed, probably could not have named him. Even bishops— who were, along with the nobility, the more direct objects of papal initiatives—experienced a remarkable degree of *de facto* autonomy. Popes did not appoint bishops (except for those dioceses that were suburbicarian sees surrounding Rome). They generally did not convene, preside over, or set the agenda for ecumenical councils. They did not canonize saints; they did not write encyclicals; they did not call bishops to Rome for regular *ad limina* visits; they were never referred to as "sovereign pontiff"; and the titles "pope" and "vicar of Christ" were used in reference not only to them but also to other bishops and even emperors. In short, throughout the first thousand years of the church, it would simply have been false to say that popes "ran the church." Church historian John O'Malley writes:

> In the early Middle Ages (and well beyond) the popes' principal duty, many believed, was to guard the tombs of the Apostles and officiate at the solemn liturgies of the great basilicas. In that period, although some of the popes of course had a broad vision of their responsibilities and dealt about weighty matters with the leaders of society, for the most part they behaved as essentially local figures, intent on local issues.[13]

This would all change in the eleventh century.

The key figure in this transformation was Pope Gregory VII (1073–1085). Pope Gregory challenged the practice of simony (the buying

[13] John W. O'Malley, "The Millennium and the Papalization of Catholicism," *America* 182, no. 12 (April 8, 2000): 14.

and selling of church offices and the sacraments) and reasserted the authority of the pope in all clerical appointments. In the eleventh century, bishops were ordinarily elected in cathedral chapters (a gathering of local church leaders) in which the nobility had come to take a prominent role. Many criticized the undue influence of the nobility on episcopal elections and controversy over these elections was common. The autonomy and integrity of local church leadership was being called into question. Pope Gregory responded dramatically to reassert his own universal jurisdiction and the proper autonomy of the bishops with a series of sweeping reforms. His intent was not the expansion of papal control *per se*, but the preservation of the bishops' authority and necessary autonomy with respect to the nobility.

Pope Gregory's ambitious reform program included measures to standardize canon law. He required that all archbishops receive the *pallium* (a vestment made of wool and worn around the neck that symbolized their pastoral role as shepherd) directly from the pope within three months of their election. He widened the use of papal legates in other countries, the authority of whom was superior to that of local bishops and metropolitans. Gregory's reforms began a new trajectory in the development of the papacy. In the centuries that followed, the title *vicarius Christi* (a title previously shared by all bishops and even kings) took on a new meaning. No longer did it convey the sense of one who was transparent to God's will and purposes as it did during the first millennium. The title was now reserved exclusively to the pope and conveyed the sense that he was an earthly surrogate for Christ.[14] Pope Gregory's reforms may have had as their purpose the preservation of the autonomy of the church, however, as William Henn has observed, "one may wonder whether the juridical means used to achieve this end may not have overshadowed the desired effect. The desired freedom was won, but the fundamental 'sacramentality' of the church was somewhat forgotten in the face of the overriding insistence that the church is a juridically structured society."[15] From this point on the papacy was

---

[14] Yves Congar, "Titres donnés au pape," in *Concilium* 108 (1975): 55–64.

[15] William Henn, *The Honor of My Brothers: A Brief History of the Relationship Between the Pope and the Bishops* (New York: Crossroad, 2000), 107–8.

"no longer merely the center and bond of unity, but the very source and origin of all churches."[16]

The upshot of the Gregorian reforms was the solidification of all ecclesiastical authority in the papacy. As the centuries progressed, the papacy gradually appropriated imperial trappings as it engaged in an increasingly competitive relationship with emperors and monarchs. The practice of papal coronations was established during this period and imperial seals began to appear on papal thrones. This increase in papal authority was buttressed by the influence of the Christian Neoplatonism of Pseudo-Dionysius on thirteenth- and fourteenth-century medieval ecclesiology. Many of the medievals conceived the church as a mirror of the celestial "hierarchy." Within this pyramidal view of the church, the pope was granted the *plenitudo potestatis*, the fullness of power.

The late fourteenth and early fifteenth centuries saw the Western church racked by schism. Widespread ecclesiastical corruption and a series of incompetent popes led to a situation in which, by the end of the fourteenth century, there were first two and then three claimants to the papal throne. This tragic situation led to the convocation of the Council of Constance in 1413, considered the greatest (at least in terms of representation) ecclesiastical assembly of the entire Middle Ages. This council agreed that the only viable solution was the resignation of all three claimants. The council's dramatic action, however, suggested to some that an ecumenical council had an authority independent of the papacy. Indeed, in 1415 the council promulgated the controversial decree *Haec sancta* that claimed, among other things, the supremacy of a council regarding matters of faith. The precise interpretation of this decree is a matter of some dispute. While some canonists saw in it a clear assertion of a council's primacy over the pope, others took a more moderate view, holding that the decree affirmed only that a legitimately constituted council derived its authority not from the pope but from Christ and, therefore, its teachings could command the obedience of all the faithful, including the pope.

The more extreme conciliarist position led to an inevitable backlash. In the early fifteenth century, the Council of Florence offered

---

[16] Klaus Schatz, *Papal Primacy: From Its Origins to the Present* (Collegeville, MN: Liturgical Press, 1996), 86.

a muscular reassertion of the authority of the pope over councils, and, from that time on, any effort to assert even the limited regional autonomy of local bishops was viewed as an attack on the authority of the papacy and condemned as a new form of conciliarism. In the late fifteenth and early sixteenth centuries, figures such as John of Torquemada and Cajetan wrote treatises asserting a profoundly monarchial vision of the papacy. Cajetan, for example, insists in his treatise *De comparatione auctoritatis Papae et Concilii* (1511) that Christ made Peter alone his vicar with all the other apostles deriving their authority from St. Peter.

In the sixteenth century, the Council of Trent was convened to respond to the challenges of various Protestant Reformers. The post-Tridentine church, eager to respond to the Reformation emphasis on an invisible church, gave unprecedented emphasis to the church as a visible society. For example, St. Robert Bellarmine reacted to the Reformers' denigration of the visible church by insisting that ecclesial institutions were integral to the very definition of the church: "The church is a gathering of persons which is as visible and palpable as the gathering of the people of Rome, the kingdom of Gaul, or the Republic of Venice."[17] The unintended consequence was, as Yves Congar put it, an ecclesiology reduced to "a defense and affirmation of the reality of the Church as machinery of hierarchical mediation, or of the power and primacy of the Roman see, in a word, a 'hierarchology.' "[18]

At the heart of this emerging "hierarchology," or what I have called the hierocratic form, was the rapid development of the bureaucratic apparatus of the papacy. In 1588, Pope Sixtus V set about a comprehensive reform of the Roman Curia. He established various congregations or dicasteries, each with specifically assigned responsibilities for the welfare of the church. This diluted the authority of the whole College of Cardinals as an independent body that might be able to challenge the pope. It also created a massive bureaucracy that would serve as a successful instrument in furthering papal policy and

---

[17] Robert Bellarmine, *De Conciliis, et Ecclesia, De Controversiis: Christianae Fidei Adversus Haereticos* (Rome: Giunchi et Menicanti, 1836), 2: bk. 3, chap. 2, p. 90.

[18] Yves, Congar, *Lay People in the Church*, rev. ed. (London: Geoffrey Chapman, 1985), 45.

unifying church practice. During a period that saw the emergence of many national monarchies, the papacy began to organize itself according to such a monarchical model. In spite of these centralizing forces, up to the French Revolution the church remained, from the perspective of organizational polity, "a federal body," with bishops retaining significant authority within their local churches.

A more profound ecclesial shift transpired in the wake of the French Revolution and its unprecedented attack on the French church. The papacy was impotent to do anything in response to this virulent antichurch program. In 1798 the pope was ignominiously taken prisoner by French troops and died a year later. That same year saw the publication of a treatise by a Camaldolese monk named Mauro Cappellari that vigorously defended the prerogatives of the papacy. The book was titled *The Triumph of the Holy See and the Church over the Attacks of Innovators, Who Are Rejected and Fought with Their Own Weapons*, and in it Cappellari offered an impassioned defense of unfettered papal authority. He argued for the absolute authority of the papacy based on the analogy of the sovereign authority of the state. The substance of his sweeping claims to papal authority took on a greater significance when, in 1831, Cappellari was elected as Pope Gregory XVI. He would soon enact a reform program known as Ultramontanism (an ecclesial attitude that looked "beyond the mountains," that is, the Alps, to ascertain Rome's views on a matter) that dramatically enhanced papal centralization.

The challenges to papal authority were hardly limited to France. Throughout much of the nineteenth century, the papacy would struggle against a growing Italian nationalism and the potential loss of the Papal States. Italian unity was finally achieved in the war against Austria in 1859–1860, forcing Rome, under Gregory's successor, Pope Pius IX, to give up two-thirds of its papal territories. Only the intercession of Napoleon III and the disposition of a French garrison in Rome allowed the papacy to maintain control of the territory immediately surrounding the city of Rome.

Many Catholics viewed the plight of the pope with sympathy and easily equated papal "sovereignty" in the temporal order with papal authority. At the First Vatican Council, convened in 1869, the bishops were eager to demonstrate their support for the pope. Vatican I issued a constitution, *Pastor aeternus*, that solemnly defined both papal primacy and infallibility. The council had intended to issue another document offering a more comprehensive treatment of the church, but the council was suspended because of the Franco-Prussian War and the draft was never considered.

Even though both the German bishops and John Henry Newman argued, in the wake of *Pastor aeternus*, that Vatican I did *not* grant the pope unfettered authority, the practical impact of Vatican I's teaching was a further enhanced papo-centric vision of the church.[19] The end of the nineteenth century and the beginning of the twentieth would be marked by a curious irony: the loss of virtually all temporal authority (with the Lateran Treaty in 1929 the Catholic Church would eventually be granted the small tract of land that is now Vatican City) led to an unprecedented increase in the pope's spiritual authority. The encyclical, which first emerged as a papal instrument of instruction in the eighteenth century, would soon become an indispensable tool for the expansion of the pope's doctrinal teaching authority. In 1950, Pope Pius XII would assert in *Humani Generis* that even when a pope pronounced on a matter in his noninfallible, ordinary magisterium, that matter was no longer subject to free theological debate.[20] That same year the pope solemnly defined the bodily Assumption of Mary, the last pope to make an *ex cathedra* dogmatic pronouncement. The pontificate of Pius XII marked, in many ways, the apotheosis of the monarchial papacy and the achievement of a thoroughly papo-centric church leadership structure.

The brief but influential pontificate of Pope St. John XXIII, marked by his audacious decision to convene the first ecumenical council in ninety years, promised a new direction for the papacy. His successor, Pope Paul VI, helped bring the council to a successful conclusion

---

[19] See the 1875 Statement of the German Bishops, "Collective Declaration of the German Episcopate on the Circular of the Imperial German Chancellor concerning the Next Papal Election." An English translation of this statement can be found in Hans Küng, *The Council and Reunion* (London: Sheed and Ward, 1961), 283–95. Newman's response is found in his famous *A Letter Addressed to His Grace the Duke of Norfolk: On Occasion of Mr. Gladstone's Recent Expostulation* (London: B. M. Pickering, 1875).

[20] Pius XII, *Humani Generis*, par. 20. This document is available online at: http://w2.vatican.va/content/pius-xii/en/encyclicals/documents/hf_p-xii _enc_12081950_humani-generis.html.

and made a number of tentative efforts to implement the council's teaching. The effectiveness of his pontificate, however, was in many ways compromised by a fear of schism. Pope Paul VI saw his ministry as that of maintaining a balancing act, often by making important concessions to the Curia. In his memoirs, Archbishop Rembert Weakland wrote:

> As I analyzed the situation in which Paul found himself, I concluded that the dominant motivation behind much of what he did in that post-conciliar period could be found in his conviction that he had to reach out to the curial and other conservative cardinals. . . . The slight alterations he made on his own to the documents already approved by the bishops at Vatican II, like the one on ecumenism and the *Nota Praevia* . . . and the bold decision to take the question of contraception out of the hands of the council to write his own document—all these uncharacteristic acts were aimed at placating the conservative cardinals who feared he might betray the First Vatican Council (1870) and its definition of papal infallibility, key to the pope's role as they saw it.[21]

Weakland contended that even after the council, Pope Paul tried to keep the peace by way of counterbalancing appointments. He would often appoint prefects and secretaries of major dicasteries with opposing views. Sometimes he would create parallel bodies to accomplish this balancing act, like the creation of the Pontifical Council for Peace and Justice to counterbalance the more pragmatic Secretariat of State.

The pontificate of Pope St. John Paul II, the first non-Italian pope in over four hundred years, began with great promise. He boldly pursued select trajectories of conciliar teaching, particularly as regards dialogue with world religions, religious freedom, and the need for a more constructive relationship between religion and science. In spite of his many considerable achievements, his concrete exercise of papal authority marked, in many ways, a return to the pontificate of Pius XII. Like his preconciliar predecessor, John Paul II had no patience for theological disagreement with authoritative church teaching. A number of theologians were disciplined over the course of his pontificate. He greatly enhanced papal authority through an unprecedented expansion of the papal canonization of saints and through a significant weaken-

---

[21] Rembert G. Weakland, *Pilgrim in a Pilgrim Church: Memoirs of a Catholic Archbishop* (Grand Rapids, MI: Eerdmans, 2009), 215.

ing of the authority of episcopal conferences. Under his watch, a universal catechism was promulgated that discouraged more regional and inculturated expressions of the Catholic faith. His charismatic personality often played into a postmodern culture of spectacle. His successor, Pope Benedict XVI, pursued a more subdued public persona but maintained the same heavy-handed exercise of papal authority and suspicion of postconciliar collegial structures like episcopal conferences. In the spring of 2013, as Pope Benedict XVI undertook the remarkable act of resigning from papal office, the papacy remained in many ways, a thoroughly monarchial institution.

III. A Sacral Priesthood

The gradual emergence of a sacral priesthood represents the third pillar in the hierocratic form of the church.[22] By *sacral* priesthood I mean not only a particular theological rationale for the ministerial priesthood but also a set of attitudes and practices associated with the priesthood. The sacral priesthood conceives of the priest as a minister ordained to a clerical elite, separate from the rest of the people of God, superior in holiness and wisdom, and granted exclusive responsibility for all teaching and ministry in the church. I can only briefly consider here a few historical factors that contributed to the emergence of this sacral priesthood. Many of these reach back into the first millennium, even though they do not really coalesce into a central pillar of the hierocratic ecclesial form until early in the second millennium.

A first development came as the result of a dramatic hardening of the distinction between the clergy and the laity, beginning in the fourth century.[23] More and more ministries, many of which had once been exercised by the laity, were now reserved for clerics. These

[22] Here I borrow the term used by Lafont to describe an element in what he described as the "Gregorian form of the church." See Lafont, *Imagining the Catholic Church*, 56–64.

[23] Alexandre Faivre, *Les laïcs aux origines de l'Eglise* (Paris: Centurion, 1984); English translation: *The Emergence of the Laity in the Early Church* (New York: Paulist Press, 1990).

diverse ministries, over time, would be reconfigured as an ascending ladder of ecclesiastical ranks, what is sometimes termed the *cursus honorum*.[24] In the medieval church of Rome, this *cursus honorum* took the following form: porter, lector, exorcist, acolyte (the minor orders), followed by subdeacon, deacon, presbyter, and bishop (the major orders). Lost was the sense of a plurality of ministries exercised by a multitude of the faithful for the building up of the church and in the service of the church's mission.

A second development accompanied the first, namely, the gradual sacerdotalization of the priesthood. There is considerable evidence of emerging public ministries in the New Testament church, but there is no explicit theology of a ministerial *priesthood*. We do find in the New Testament a minority tradition that affirms the priesthood of Christ in the Letter to the Hebrews. In 1 Peter the entire church is affirmed as a priestly people. This biblical testimony, of course, does not negate the legitimate growth in the church's understanding of its ordained ministry and its gradual recognition that the bishop and eventually the presbyter would exercise a distinctly priestly ministry. So we can recognize in the early centuries a sense that in the Eucharist, a priestly people gathered at the table of the Lord under the presidency of a bishop who exercised a *primatum sacerdotium* (a "high" or "first priesthood"). Unfortunately, by the fifth and sixth centuries, the priestly character of all the baptized was obscured and priesthood was located exclusively in the bishop as the "head priest" and the presbyters who now shared in that ministry as "secondary priests."[25]

A third factor was the consequence of a momentous debate regarding the theology of the Eucharist that began in the ninth century. Prior to the ninth century, it was commonly accepted that the celebration of the Eucharist effected a twofold transformation of bread and wine into the body and blood of Christ and the transformation of the gathered community into the ecclesial body of Christ. In the

---

[24] See John St. H. Gibaut, *The* Cursus Honorum: *A Study of Origins and Evolution of Sequential Ordination*, Patristic Studies, vol. 3 (Bern: Peter Lang, 2000).

[25] James F. Puglisi, "Presider as *Alter Christus*, Head of the Body?," *Liturgical Ministry* 10 (Summer 2001): 153–58, at 154. For a more in-depth documentation of this shift, see James F. Puglisi, *The Process of Admission to Ordained Ministry*, vol. 1, *Epistemological Principles and Roman Catholic Rites* (Collegeville, MN: Liturgical Press, 1996).

ninth century, a protracted dispute began regarding precisely how and in what manner the elements of bread and wine were transformed into the body and blood of Christ.[26]

This singular focus on the transformation of the eucharistic *elements* led to a gradual neglect of the transformation of the eucharistic *community*. With Eucharist and church no longer closely related, ministry involving one need not involve the other. This separation is reflected in the growing significance of the canonical distinction between the power of orders (*potestas ordinis*) and the power of jurisdiction (*potestas iurisdictionis*).[27] That is, it was increasingly possible to ordain one to sacramental ministry apart from pastoral leadership of a living eucharistic community. The consequence was a shift away from ordained ministry conceived as service to a community and toward ordained ministry conceived as the exercise of sacramental power. The priesthood would now be understood almost exclusively as the power to confect the Eucharist and absolve sins with no substantive reference to a concrete local church.

A fourth factor in the rise of a sacral priesthood emerges in the seventeenth century with the "French School" of spirituality led by Pierre de Bérulle, St. Jean Eudes, and St. Vincent de Paul.[28] The French School was intent on reforming a corrupt priesthood by way of a renewed emphasis on the holiness of the priest. Here the priest is presented as an *alter Christus*, "another Christ." In other words, he represents Christ through his interior holiness and the offering of the holy sacrifice of the Eucharist. This new spirituality offered a fruitful resource for the reform and renewal of the priesthood but it also risked reducing priestly identity to one essential moment, when the priest pronounces the words of institution. The priest represented Christ not in his action or service on behalf of the kingdom

---

[26] The classic study of this shift in the theology of the Eucharist and its implications for ecclesiology is Henri de Lubac, *Corpus Mysticum: l'eucharistie et l'Église au Moyen âge. Étude historique* (Paris: Aubier, 1949); English translation, *Corpus Mysticum: The Eucharist and the Church in the Middle Ages; Historical Survey* (Notre Dame, IN: University of Notre Dame Press, 2006).

[27] See Laurent Villemin, *Pouvoir d'ordre et pouvoir de juridiction: Histoire théologique de leur distinction* (Paris: Cerf, 2003).

[28] Maurice Vidal, "Presbyterat," in *Dictionnaire de spiritualité* (Paris: Beauchesne, 1985), 2093–94.

but in his very being. The Oratorians, Vincentians, and Sulpicians effectively disseminated this priestly spirituality through their many seminaries established throughout the world. Indeed, for much of the first half of the twentieth century, priests were nourished on a classic expression of this spirituality in Dom Marmion's *Christ: The Ideal of the Priest.*[29] An overlooked curiosity regarding this development is the surprising paucity of theological reflection on the ministry of the priest in the light of the life and ministry of Jesus of Nazareth. In the literature of this period, the priest acted "in the person of Christ" primarily as the one offering sacrifice, not as the one who fed the hungry, healed the sick, offered solace to the discouraged, and washed the feet of his disciples.

The result of these historical developments was a profile of the sacral priest that dominated the Catholic imagination on the eve of the council: a holy man shorn of his sexuality, possessing distinctive sacramental powers and unquestioned ecclesiastical authority.

IV. A Mechanistic Theology of Grace and the Sacraments

From the very beginning of Christianity, the sacramental life of the church played a central role in Christian discipleship and offered a privileged participation in the life of grace. Of course, neither the biblical testimony nor the documentary witness of the first several centuries of Christianity offers us anything like a systematic theology of grace and sacraments. The Latin *gratia* translated the Greek *charis*. Both were used as a noun and adjective to articulate how God's redeeming love was encountered concretely in the Christian life. Again, we cannot hope to offer anything like a history of the theology of grace and the sacramental life of the church. All that is possible is a brief marking out of important transitions over the course of church history that eventually contributed to the hierocratic form.

In the Eastern Church, grace was considered in the light of a view of the human person created in the image and likeness of God. Within this scheme, sin represented a dramatic defacing of that divine image. Christ came to heal this defaced image and to restore our capacity

---

[29] Columba Marmion, *Christ: The Ideal of the Priest* (St. Louis: Herder, 1952).

for divine communion. Christ came, in other words, to *divinize* us. Grace referred to the action of Christ divinizing the believer by way of mystical union and thereby making possible a transformed relationship with God. The sacraments were ritual participations in this process of spiritual transformation.

For much of the first thousand years in the Western church, grace was understood within the drama of the human capacity to love and sin understood as a rejection of that invitation. St. Augustine, that great fourth- and fifth-century bishop and theologian, offered a theology of grace and sacraments that would dominate the church for centuries to come. For Augustine, love was the act whereby we commit ourselves to one thing and not to another. It is this act of choosing, this act of the will, which brings us happiness. The task of the Christian life is to order the will, the seat of love, to choose properly. Thus Augustine could say: *dilige et quod vis fac* ("love, and do what you will").[30]

Yet here we encounter a fundamental difficulty, for Augustine, reflecting on his own experience, found that it was impossible for humans to properly order our loving. Our wills were so wounded by sin that we were unable to choose God. This is not simply the result of our own sinfulness, however. It is through Adam's disobedience that we have inherited a disordered will; a will that is in bondage to the flesh. This bondage leads us to further sin. Grace is thus conceived as a dramatic, divine force encountered particularly through the sacraments that liberates us from the bondage of sin and heals us of all that prevents us from the life of love.

Early Christianity, both East and West, developed within a cultural milieu heavily indebted to Platonism. In a Platonic world, that which was most "real" was the spiritual realm of eternal ideas and forms. All created things find their true meaning and significance within the spiritual realm. What we today might call sense data could be trusted only to the extent that it was seen as sharing in or participating in the spiritual world. This goes against our modern instinct to put our trust in empirical sensory data. If we can see it and touch it, it must be real. Early Christian thought went in a quite different direction. Thus, over much of the first thousand years, the sacramental life

---

[30] Augustine, *Sermon 7*, on *1 John*.

of the church was understood simply as a symbolic participation in the spiritual realm. A deep sacramental consciousness came easily within a Platonic milieu.

The next great transition in the Christian understanding of the life of grace and the sacraments came in the thirteenth century with the contributions of St. Thomas Aquinas.[31] Whereas Augustine was shaped by the inheritance of the philosophy of Plato, this Dominican friar drew insight from the contributions of yet another ancient Greek philosopher, Aristotle. If Plato understood all created reality as fundamentally dependent on the spiritual realm of eternal forms, Aristotle emphasized the relative autonomy of created realities. Thomas drew on the contributions of Aristotle and recognized that all creatures have a distinctive created nature that allows them to be what they are. This is the case for humans as well, yet humans, Thomas insists, can access a spiritual dimension (the realm of grace) that does not compete with their natural existence but rather brings it to its perfection. Thus, where Augustine thought of grace in the light of the reality of human sinfulness, Thomas thought of grace as the perfection and elevation of human nature so as to make possible friendship with God. In this regard Thomas distinguished between *uncreated* grace, the very power and love of God itself, and *created* grace, as the concrete effects of grace in the life of the believer. The sacraments provide believers with the ordinary means for entering into and enhancing their graced friendship with God.

In the late Middle Ages the theological breakdown of this Thomistic understanding of grace, widespread corruption in the administration of the sacraments, and a poorly educated clergy combined to produce a church in which popular sacramental practice and sound theological understandings of that practice were widely separated. That late medieval world was susceptible to stringent theological critique of the kind offered by the sixteenth-century Reformers like Martin Luther and John Calvin. Although, in many quarters of the

---

[31] My Franciscan friends and colleagues will have to forgive me for not giving the Franciscan tradition of St. Bonaventure and Duns Scotus, for reasons of space, the attention it properly deserves.

church, a vital Catholic sacramental life continued to thrive,[32] the Reformers had correctly identified numerous abuses in the church's liturgical and sacramental life. They criticized what appeared to be a magical understanding of the sacraments, an excessive preoccupation with the intercession of the saints who functioned like feudal patrons, a clericalization of Christian worship, and a diminution of the active participation of all the baptized in the Eucharist. Some, like Ulrich Zwingli, presented more radical challenges, sweeping away the entire Catholic sacramental system.

The force and scope of these attacks put the late medieval church on the defensive. The Council of Trent, which met intermittently between 1545 and 1563, sought in its own way to address many of the abuses in Catholicism that had raised the ire of the Reformers, even as it defended church teaching from its more extreme detractors. In 1562, the council issued a decree that addressed many of the abuses that had been criticized by the Reformers. Trent instigated a postconciliar liturgical/sacramental reform that relied on the standardization of Catholic worship and the suppression of liturgical diversity in favor of a sweeping regimen that enforced uniformity in liturgical practice.

This program to establish widespread uniformity in liturgical practice led to a comprehensive reform of the church's liturgical books and the extensive codification of liturgical rules, or rubrics. New printing technologies allowed for a rapid dissemination of these liturgical books throughout the whole church. The period between the seventeenth and twentieth centuries witnesses a growing preoccupation with liturgical rubrics that would govern virtually every aspect of Catholic liturgical life.[33] It was not long before determinations of the very efficacy or validity of church sacraments were viewed in the light of these rubrics. To violate the slightest rule put the efficacy of the sacraments in jeopardy. This new attention to liturgical rubrics was accompanied by a shift in the Catholic theology of grace.

---

[32] See, for example, the illuminating study of Eamon Duffy, *The Stripping of the Altars: Traditional Religion in England c. 1400–c. 1580* (New Haven, CT: Yale University Press, 2005).

[33] Pierre Jounel, "From the Council of Trent to Vatican Council II," in *The Church at Prayer*, vol. 1: *Principles of the Liturgy*, ed. A. G. Mortimort (Collegeville, MN: Liturgical Press, 1992), 63–84.

For much of church history, grace was understood in the light of the working of the Holy Spirit in the life of believers. As we saw above, for Thomas Aquinas the primary understanding of grace was that of uncreated grace, the indwelling of the Holy Spirit in the life of Christians that made possible friendship with God. In the period after the Reformation, grace is less frequently understood as the indwelling of God in the believer (uncreated grace) or as the spiritual life principle which by baptism becomes a permanent, created feature of our Christian existence (*habitual* grace). Instead, emphasis is placed on *actual* grace, a special, transitory force which is occasional in nature and which moves us through our emotions and our will to do what is right. Baroque Catholicism was marked by the flourishing of this theology of grace, with its emphasis on the particular actions and manifestations of God's activity in the church and world. It was reflected in the bold ministerial activism of so many new professed religious communities. It found expression in active spiritualities like that championed by St. Ignatius Loyola and the Society of Jesus, which emphasized the importance of finding God in all things.

This baroque theology of grace could, however, also be distorted. Too often during this period, actual grace became almost "thingified," overshadowing uncreated grace and habitual grace. On the eve of Vatican II, Catholics certainly experienced the sacraments as a source of nourishment for spiritual growth. An emphasis on the correct performance of liturgical rubrics, however, and an understanding of grace as spiritual "stuff" could, and often did, devolve into a sacramental spirituality in which the sacraments functioned as automatic grace dispensers.

V. A Confrontational Attitude toward the World

The final pillar of the hierocratic form was the construction of Roman Catholicism as a kind of Catholic counter-society in response to a world viewed as hostile to the church and its mission. The history of the church's relationship with the world is again so complex that it will only be possible here to mark out a few basic shifts in the church/world relationship over the course of two millennia of church history.

Early Christianity harbored an imminent expectation of Christ's return that led to a markedly hostile attitude toward the world. For early Christians, conversion to the faith required a considerable social relocation; it meant changing the group within which the believer identified him- or herself. In sociological terms, Christian conversion brought one into a new primary reference group. It was common for early Christians to refer to themselves as constituting a new *genos*, that is, a new race or nation. Even the opponents of Christianity referred to Christians derisively as a "third race," neither Greek nor Jew, but something else altogether different.[34] Origen, that great third-century thinker from Alexandria, wrote: "But we know of the existence in each city of another sort of country, created by the Logos of God."[35] This "other country" was, of course, the church.

Much of this would change with the fourth-century Constantinian settlement that ended the sporadic persecution of Christians in the Roman Empire. The church was called into an uneasy partnership with the state.[36] This rapprochement was not universally welcomed. For example, Augustine would take a cautious stance toward the church's cooperation with the powers of this world and particularly with the state. Augustine will address this dilemma in his famous work, *The City of God*. The great North African bishop walked a fine line, asserting on the one hand that it was possible for Christians to participate in civil community while still relativizing the value of that civil society in comparison to church life. Augustine posited a secular realm in which there was a real contestation between Christian and pagan values.[37]

Others took an even more pessimistic view of the possibility of a Christian's participation in civil society. Early Christian hermits

[34] Wayne A. Meeks, *The Origins of Christian Morality: The First Two Centuries* (New Haven, CT: Yale University Press, 1993), 9.

[35] Origen, *Contra Celsum*, trans. Henry Chadwick (Cambridge, UK: Cambridge University Press, 1953), 510.

[36] Space limitations prohibit our consideration of the very different configurations of the church/world relationship in Byzantium or in the development of Christianity in the Eastern orbit of Armenia, Syria, India, or, for that matter, in Ethiopian Africa.

[37] My reading of St. Augustine here is indebted to Robert A. Markus, *Christianity and the Secular* (Notre Dame, IN: University of Notre Dame Press, 2006).

and monastic groups, particularly in the fourth and fifth centuries, deliberately withdrew from what they viewed as a hostile world. Thomas Merton aptly describes this movement, writing of a group of hermits known as the "Desert Fathers":

> Society . . . was regarded by them as a shipwreck from which each single individual man had to swim for his life. . . . These were men who believed that to let oneself drift along, passively accepting the tenets and values of what they knew as society was purely and simply a disaster. The fact that the Emperor was now Christian and that the "world" was coming to know the Cross as a sign of temporal power only strengthened them in their resolve.[38]

As the Western church moved into the Middle Ages, it further implicated itself in a feudal culture, establishing an ecclesial and geopolitical reality known as Christendom that sustained an uneasy partnership of church and empire. Within this partnership, popes and emperors sparred for supremacy.

The Reformation rent asunder the precious unity of the Western church of the Middle Ages. The rise of modern science in the work of Copernicus, Galileo, Kepler, and Newton presented an unprecedented challenge to the authority of the church, as did the Enlightenment with its celebration of autonomous human reason. We must add to this the virulent anticlericalism of the French Revolution that marked the beginning of a series of political revolutions over the next seventy-five years that abolished, at least temporarily, a number of church-supported monarchies.

In the nineteenth century, church authorities issued more and more ecclesiastical pronouncements on "worldly affairs." Popes would condemn unwarranted state interference in church matters and would repeatedly insist that the state had an obligation to preserve the right of Catholics to practice their faith. In Western Europe, the late eighteenth and early nineteenth centuries saw dramatic social developments occasioned by the rise of industrialism and dramatic population shifts from rural areas to the cities. The church was quick to recognize the potentially dangerous social consequences

---

[38] Thomas Merton, *The Wisdom of the Desert* (New York: New Directions, 1960), 3.

of these developments. While the anticlericalism of the French Revolution abated to an extent, the tumultuous events of the nineteenth century only exacerbated the church's defensive posture toward a world perceived as increasingly hostile to the church. Pope Gregory XVI produced a series of condemnations of modern liberalism, and Pope Pius IX, initially open to the liberal impulse, was shocked by the wave of nationalist revolutions that swept Western Europe in 1848 and took up Gregory's substantial repudiation of liberalism.

With the pontificate of Leo XIII in the late nineteenth century, the church embarked on a more positive, if still quite cautious, engagement with the issues of the larger world. Yet this stance was short-lived. The violent reaction to modernism early in the pontificate of Pope Pius X reinforced key elements of the siege mentality preponderant since the Reformation. A confrontational stance toward society continued in the first half of the twentieth century with the papacy issuing sharp rebukes of significant elements of modern capitalism, socialism, industrialism, and a continued program of state encroachment in church matters. The specific formulation of Catholic social teaching would be warranted by ever-more expansive claims to papal authority in the affairs of the world. It would be left for the pontificate of John XXIII and the Second Vatican Council to reconceive the church's relationship to the larger world.

In this chapter I have provided a brief outline of the emergence of key components or "pillars" contributing to the hierocratic form of the church. This ecclesial form was the result of centuries of development. It bears repeating that a negative judgment of the adequacy of this ecclesial form does not require that we deny its positive features. Many Catholics found life within the hierocratic form of the church meaningful and fulfilling. In the United States, for example, parishes often provided a rich sense of community, sustained as they were by the various parochial schools, sodalities, and other parish-based voluntary associations. These parish communities sustained a thick sense of Catholic identity that helped hand on the Catholic tradition. This Catholic culture produced strong families, encouraged frequent celebrations of the sacraments, and provided religious education that genuinely influenced peoples' lives. Limiting our reflections here to the US Catholic context, however, it was unclear whether the Catholic life the hierocratic form encouraged was sustainable in the modern world.

By the 1930s, cracks began to appear in the thick Catholic culture of ghetto Catholicism. The work of Catholic social theorists like John A. Ryan demonstrated the applicability of Catholic social teaching to American political and economic issues. The Great Depression drew Catholics into larger debates about the welfare of American society.[39] In the wake of World War II, many immigrant Catholics became much more conscious of their American identity. In a quite different key, countercultural proponents of what might be called radical Catholicism, like Dorothy Day and the Catholic Worker movement, encouraged Catholics to emerge from their immigrant enclosures and challenge key features of the American settlement in the light of their Catholic faith. The American Jesuit John Courtney Murray demonstrated the possibility of a rapprochement between Catholic teaching and the American constitutional principle of separation of church and state. All of this simply reinforced the social factors that emerged in the wake of World War II that were inexorably dismantling the American Catholic subculture. As Jay Dolan has pointed out,

> even if Vatican II had never happened, the renewal of Catholicism would still have taken place in the United States. That is because the social and cultural transformation of the post–World War II era proved to be as important if not indeed more important for American Catholics than Vatican II.[40]

These social and cultural tectonic shifts taking place below the surface of American Catholicism tracked closely with similar developments in Western Europe. Together they provided the backdrop to the more explicitly ecclesiological shifts associated with the Second Vatican Council.

Although it is unlikely that any of the bishops would have explicitly described their efforts as a reaction to a "hierocratic form of the church," they were clearly responding to perceived inadequacies in Catholic theology, discipline, and practice at the midpoint of the

---

[39] Jay P. Dolan, *In Search of an American Catholicism* (New York: Oxford University Press, 2002), 152.

[40] Ibid., 189.

twentieth century. In short, the bishops recognized the shortcomings of the ecclesial *status quo*. This led them to a more discerning reading of "the signs of the times" and a creative appropriation of neglected elements of the great tradition. The result, whether the bishops were explicitly aware of it or not, was the partial construction of an alternative form of the church, one more capable of addressing the challenges of the modern age.

We are now in a position to consider the council's response to the inadequacies of the hierocratic form. Part of that response was embodied not just in the documents the council produced but in its very conduct. The ecclesial dynamics at work at the council suggested a new way of being church. The council's singular achievement is justly celebrated today, but few can appreciate how perilous was the work of the council and how close the council came to disaster. A study of the forces and conciliar dynamics that redirected the council away from its perilous beginnings has as much to teach the church today as a study of the council's documents. It is to that remarkable story that we must turn in the next chapter.

2

The Council
That Almost Failed

On January 25, 1959, at the Basilica of St. Paul-Outside-the-Walls, newly elected Pope St. John XXIII gathered with a small group of cardinals. The context of the meeting was the celebration of vespers for the conclusion of the Week of Prayer for Christian Unity. At that meeting, the elderly pope announced his intention to convene a new ecumenical council, the first in ninety years.

Now let us "fast-forward" more than three and a half years to August 1962, less than two months from the opening of the council. Paul-Émile Léger, cardinal-archbishop of Montreal, drafted a twelve-page letter with the accompanying signatures of Cardinals Frings, Liénart, Döpfner, Suenens, and König.[1] In that letter, he warned that without immediate papal action any hopes for real church reform would founder on the shoals of stout conservative opposition. Why was Léger so fearful that the council would fail? To answer that question, we must consider the preparatory period between the pope's daring announcement and the Léger letter.

I. Preparations for the Council: Stacking the Deck

Pope John's announcement of an upcoming council marked the beginning of well over three years of conciliar preparation. Unfortunately,

[1] The letter is discussed in Gilles Routhier, "Les réactions du cardinal Léger à la préparation de Vatican II," *Revue d'Histoire de l'Eglise de France* 80 (1994): 281–302.

there was little in this preparation that augured well for substantive reform of the church. In 1959, the pope created an antepreparatory commission headed by the Vatican Secretary of State, Cardinal Domenico Tardini. This commission's work would transpire over three phases: (1) soliciting initial proposals from curial officials, bishops, religious superiors (male only), university faculties, and theologians, (2) drawing up a rough outline of topics to be addressed based on the questionnaires, (3) proposing membership for the various preparatory commissions. The pope appointed primarily curial figures to the antepreparatory commission. These were often good and holy men, but many considered the pope's call for widespread consultation an affront to their curial leadership; it smacked of a democratic mentality that, in their view, had no place in Christ's church. From their perspective it did not make sense to ask local bishops with limited pastoral experience beyond their own diocese to offer input regarding the needs of the universal church when it was the Curia that dealt with such issues on a daily basis.

The proposals gathered from this preliminary questionnaire would provide the raw material for the proximate preparation of the council. The antepreparatory commission sent out questionnaires to 2,812 bishops, theologians, religious superiors (male only), theological faculties, and congregations of the Roman Curia. Of this number, 2,150 replied in some manner, though many were short and perfunctory. The commission then organized these responses into various categories of issues and questions that would need to be addressed by the soon to be appointed preparatory commissions. Unfortunately, many of the *vota* that were submitted were vetted by the commission and classified according to the categories of canon law and the neoscholastic manual tradition. Many of the more innovative proposals, often as not, fell through the cracks.

The final task of the antepreparatory commission was to propose membership to the ten preparatory commissions that would actually have the responsibility of drawing up draft documents to be given to the bishops for council debate. The pope then appointed the membership of the preparatory commissions based on these recommendations. This meant that, with a few noteworthy exceptions, the preparatory commissions were also placed in the hands of the leading curial officials least disposed to upset the ecclesial *status quo*.

Many bishops who were hopeful for ecclesial reform were dismayed at the way in which the pope appeared to hand over council preparation to the curial leadership. Cardinal Leo Suenens writes in his memoirs:

> In the presence of the entire group [a special steering committee created by Pope John] I asked him: "Holy Father, why did you appoint the prefects of Roman Congregations to head the Council Commissions? This can only inhibit the freedom of Council members in their work and in their discussions." He answered, laughing: "You're quite right, but I didn't have the courage."[2]

A further task of the antepreparatory commission concerned the rules of the council. In his very first press conference, Cardinal Tardini had announced that many bishops were concerned about being drawn away from their dioceses for an extended period of time. Consequently, the likely procedure would be to have preparatory texts drafted in advance of the council and then sent to the bishops for their comments. When the bishops arrived at the council, they would be in a position to go ahead and vote on these revised texts. Later, Fr. Sebastian Tromp, secretary for the Theological Commission, would come to the defense of Tardini's view, contending that it wasn't actually necessary that the bishops be physically gathered together to conduct council business to the point of arguing that it wasn't even necessary for the bishops to actually gather in one place! Paul Phillippe, a representative of the Holy Office, went so far as to propose that the bishops need not be allowed to actually speak at the council but only to offer written comments in advance and then simply cast their vote on the *schemata* at the general session. Fortunately, the views of Tromp and Philippe were quite extreme and perhaps spurred other bishops, including curialists like Archbishop Parente, to insist on the fundamental right of bishops to speak at a council.[3]

---

[2] Leó-Joseph Suenens, *Memories and Hopes* (Dublin: Veritas, 1992), 71.

[3] Joseph Komonchak, "The Struggle for the Council during the Preparation of Vatican II (1960–1962)," in *History of Vatican II*, ed. Giuseppe Alberigo and Joseph A. Komonchak (Maryknoll, NY: Orbis Books, 1995), 1:326–29.

In the summer of 1962 the pope promulgated the rules of procedure for the council as the *Ordo Concilii Oecumenici Vaticani II Celebrandi*.[4] A number of important norms were established in the *Ordo Concilii*:

- Although at Vatican I the bishops chose all the members of the conciliar commissions, the rules of Vatican II allowed the bishops to elect sixteen members, leaving eight members to be appointed by the pope.
- The *periti* for the conciliar commissions would be designated by the pope. Additionally, each bishop could bring his own *peritus* to the council. The *periti* assigned by the pope to commissions could attend the general congregations but could not speak or vote at them. The bishops' own *periti* were not allowed to attend the general congregations. At the commission meetings, *periti* could attend but could not vote and could only speak if invited to do so.
- One of the more significant rules for the council determined that the council would be conducted in its entirety in Latin.

There is some thought that this last rule was intended to put certain bishops at a disadvantage, though early in the council it became readily apparent that many of the prelates most enthusiastic about the retention of Latin in the church were not nearly as accomplished in Latin as they fancied themselves to be. The American bishops often spoke Latin with an accent that made them quite unintelligible to the Europeans and vice-versa. Edward Schillebeeckx remarked:

> Spellman and McIntyre proclaim that Latin is the *only* liturgical language, but pronounce it in such an Americanised fashion that no one understands them: the worse one's spoken Latin the more one is inclined to favour it. It is a *"status symbol"* of priest-"intellectuals" as opposed to the "idiots."[5]

---

[4] *Acta et Documenta Concilio oecumenico Vaticano II apparando; Series prima (antepreparatoria)*, vol. 2, Part 1 (Rome: Typis Polyglottis Vaticanis, 1960–1961), 434 (hereafter ADP).

[5] Edward Schillebeeckx, *The Council Notes of Edward Schillebeeckx 1962–1963*, ed. Karim Schelkens (Leuven: Peeters, 2011), 13.

One person who flouted the Latin rule was one of the great cantankerous figures of the council, Maximos IV Saigh, patriarch of the Melkite rite. For him the law requiring the use of Latin was an affront to the Eastern Catholic churches, and so, when he offered his first intervention, in spite of the protestations of the president of the assembly, he delivered the entire speech in French, after which he received an ovation from the assembly!

In August, the bishops were sent the seven schemata they were to consider at the beginning of the council. Many bishops complained about receiving the schemata at such a late date and only 10 percent responded with comments.[6] The responses were overwhelmingly negative. Many of the episcopal responses were grounded in work done by leading theologians. Karl Rahner and several other German theologians met with Cardinal Döpfner and other members of the German episcopate, offering an extensive critique of the documents. Yves Congar also distributed detailed criticisms. Edward Schillebeeckx penned a response on behalf of the Dutch bishops that urged that the first four schemata be completely rewritten.[7]

Yet another shocking feature of the conciliar preparations was the fact that there was, in the midst of all of the preparations for the council, no concrete plan for how the council would conduct its business, what documents it would address, and in which order. By early 1962, the preparatory commissions had produced over seventy schemata. Cardinal Suenens, a close confidant of the pope and heavily involved in preparations for the council, and Cardinal Montini, archbishop of Milan and Pope John's eventual successor, were concerned that the council was likely to get bogged down in all of these often technical documents on items of little interest to the church at large. The Belgian primate, Cardinal Suenens, met with the pope in March 1962 to voice his concerns. Suenens asked the pope,

---

[6] Klaus Wittstadt, "On the Eve of the Second Vatican Council (July 1–October 10, 1962)," *History of Vatican II*, ed. Giuseppe Alberigo and Joseph A. Komonchak (Maryknoll, NY: Orbis Books, 1995), 1:419ff.

[7] Ibid., 425–26.

"Who is working on an overall plan for the Council?"

"Nobody," said Pope John.

"But there will be total chaos. How do you imagine we can discuss seventy-two *schemata* . . . ?"

"Yes," John agreed, "we need a plan. . . . Would you like to do one?"[8]

This was a rather delicate matter. The pope certainly agreed that an overall plan was needed, but he did not wish to appear as if he was imposing his will on the wishes of all the bishops. Consequently, the pope also asked Suenens to discuss his plans with Cardinals Montini, Döpfner, Siri, and Liénart. The pope directed Suenens: "Bring them together so that I will be able to say, 'According to the wishes of a number of cardinals,' while being a bit vague on the details. Then it won't just look like something I've cooked up."[9]

With that, Suenens drafted a pastoral plan for the council that provided some important criteria for determining what the council should and should not address. This document was submitted to the pope and, on May 19, Cardinal Amleto Cicognani, then secretary of state, sent a copy of the plan to a number of key cardinals. Nothing further was heard of it, however, until after the opening of the council.

The three and a half years of preparation for the council were conducted under curial control that allowed Vatican officials to promulgate rules that limited the free exchange of ideas. They influenced both the membership of the preparatory commission and the topics that were assigned to each commission. Rules were promulgated that placed limits on episcopal interaction during the conciliar sessions. Mediocre texts were drafted and sent on to the bishops at the "eleventh hour," leaving little opportunity for the bishops to examine properly the texts. Consequently, it is not difficult to see why Cardinal Léger and others would warn the pope that the council could well fail to achieve the goals the pope harbored for it. All of this leads to an intriguing question: why didn't the council fail?

---

[8] Léo-Joseph Suenens, "A Plan for the Whole Council," in *Vatican II by Those Who Were There*, ed. Alberic Stacpoole (London: Chapman, 1985), 88–91.

[9] Recounted in Peter Hebblethwaite, *Pope Paul VI* (New York: Paulist Press, 1993), 301.

II. Changing the Course of the Council

The first factor in the redirection of the council came at the opening Mass on October 11, 1962. The liturgy to celebrate the opening of the council was, by today's standards, remarkable in its length. Filled with Roman ceremonial, the opening liturgy lasted over seven hours.[10] For those who remained through it all, the highlight was Pope John's remarkable address, *Gaudet Mater Ecclesia*.[11] Here, for the first time, the bishops and, indeed, through the media covering the event, the entire world heard a comprehensive articulation of the pope's hopes for the council.

Pope John's Opening Address

After some introductory comments on the historical role of ecumenical councils, Pope John offered his reasons for calling an ecumenical council. The church must bring herself "up to date where required." The pope then complained that many of his closest advisers harbored a far different view of the church's situation in the modern world. What made this ecclesiastical scolding so remarkable was that many of the advisers he had in mind, eminent curial officials such as the Prefect for the Holy Office, Cardinal Alfredo Ottaviani, who had appeared on Italian television pronouncing his expectations for the council, were sitting but a few feet away!

> In the daily exercise of our pastoral office, we sometimes have to listen, much to our regret, to voices of persons who, though burning with zeal, are not endowed with too much sense of discretion or measure. In these modern times they can see nothing but prevarication and ruin. They say that our era, in comparison with past eras, is getting worse, and they behave as though they had learned nothing from history, which is, nonetheless, the teacher of life. They behave as though at the time of former councils everything was a full triumph for the Christian idea and life and for proper religious liberty. We feel we must disagree

[10] Andrea Riccardi, "The Tumultuous Opening Days of the Council," in *History of Vatican II*, 2:14.

[11] The English translation of the pope's speech opening the council can be accessed online at http://conciliaria.com/2012/10/mother-church-rejoices-opening-address-of-john-xxiii-at-the-council/#more-2134.

with those prophets of gloom, who are always forecasting disaster, as though the end of the world were at hand. In the present order of things, Divine Providence is leading us to a new order of human relations which, by men's [and women's] own efforts and even beyond their very expectations, are directed toward the fulfillment of God's superior and inscrutable designs. And everything, even human differences, leads to the greater good of the Church.

After this remarkable upbraiding of key Vatican officials, the pope then considered one of the traditional reasons for an ecumenical council, namely, the defense of church teaching. He began with an unambiguous affirmation of the church's fidelity to its doctrinal heritage. He then insisted that church doctrine must be interpreted within a framework that considers the contemporary pastoral context for the authentic proclamation of this teaching.

In order, however, that this doctrine may influence the numerous fields of human activity, with reference to individuals, to families, and to so-cial life, it is necessary first of all that the Church should never depart from the sacred patrimony of truth received from the Fathers. But at the same time she must ever look to the present, to the new conditions and new forms of life introduced into the modern world, which have opened new avenues to the Catholic apostolate.

This in turn led to a fuller consideration of how exactly the council must treat church doctrine:

The salient point of this Council is not, therefore, a discussion of one article or another of the fundamental doctrine of the Church which has repeatedly been taught by the Fathers and by ancient and modern theologians, and which is presumed to be well known and familiar to all. For this a Council was not necessary. But from the renewed, serene, and tranquil adherence to all the teaching of the Church in its entirety and preciseness, as it still shines forth in the Acts of the Council of Trent and First Vatican Council, the Christian, Catholic, and apostolic spirit of the whole world expects a step forward toward a doctrinal penetration and a formation of consciousness in faithful and perfect conformity to the authentic doctrine, which, however, should be studied and expounded through the methods of research and through the literary forms of modern thought. The substance of the ancient doctrine of the deposit of faith is one thing, and the way in which it is presented is another.

Here we find an approach to doctrine that is quite different from the static conception so common in the neoscholastic manual tradition. According to the pope, doctrine is rooted in particular historical contexts and has to be studied "through the methods of research and through the literary forms of modern thought." Appeals to church doctrine, the pope insisted, must always be open to the possibility that a doctrine may need to be reformulated in ways more conducive to its communication in the modern age.

From this more sophisticated appeal to church doctrine, the pope then offered a critical assessment of the way in which church authority treated error in the past:

> At the outset of the Second Vatican Council, it is evident, as always, that the truth of the Lord will remain forever. We see, in fact, as one age succeeds another, that the opinions of men [and women] follow one another and exclude each other. And often errors vanish as quickly as they arise, like fog before the sun. The Church has always opposed these errors. Frequently she has condemned them with the greatest severity. Nowadays however, the Spouse of Christ prefers to make use of the medicine of mercy rather than that of severity. She considers that she meets the needs of the present day by demonstrating the validity of her teaching rather than by condemnations.

The pope did not view church teaching as a way to bludgeon those in error but as a starting point for dialogue with those who disagree with the church. The pope called for a magisterium that is fundamentally pastoral in character. He was not content to have the council offer a mere repetition of previous doctrinal formulations; what was demanded was a penetration of church doctrine in view of the pressing questions of our age. Christoph Theobald has characterized the pope's address as a commitment to "the pastorality of doctrine."[12] The council followed his lead and consistently treated doctrine as something to be authentically interpreted and faithfully applied within concrete historical, cultural, and pastoral contexts. John O'Brien observes that with the work of the council

---

[12] Christoph Theobald, "The Theological Options of Vatican II: Seeking an 'Internal' Principle of Interpretation," in *Concilium: Vatican II: A Forgotten Future*, ed. Alberto Melloni and Christoph Theobald, no. 4 (2005): 87–107.

[The] pastoral had regained its proper standing as something far more than the mere application of doctrine but as the very context from which doctrines emerge, the very condition of the possibility of doctrine, the touchstone for the validity of doctrine and the always prior and posterior praxis which doctrine at most, attempts to sum up, safeguard, and transmit.[13]

The final section of the pope's opening address turned to the unity of the church:

Unfortunately, the entire Christian family has not yet fully attained this visible unity in truth. The Catholic Church, therefore, considers it her duty to work actively so that there may be fulfilled the great mystery of that unity, which Jesus Christ invoked with fervent prayer from His heavenly Father on the eve of His sacrifice.

There is a quite provocative claim embedded in this frank acknowledgment of church division. The pope could admit that the "Christian family" had not fully attained visible unity only on the assumption that non-Catholic Christians were part of that family. This new ecumenical starting point was difficult to reconcile with Pope Pius XI's exhortation in 1928 to dissident non-Catholics: "The union of Christians can only be promoted by promoting the return to the one true Church of Christ of those who are separated from it, for in the past they have unhappily left it."[14]

It is difficult to exaggerate the impact of the pope's opening address on the bishops. Numerous bishops remarked on it in their memoirs. There is a sense in which the pope opened up for the bishops a broader vision of what might be possible at this council.

Electing the Conciliar Commissions

If Pope John's address on October 11 played a dramatic role in redirecting the course of the council, a second influential event occurred but forty-eight hours later on October 13, 1962. This was the first general congregation of the council and the first order of business was the elec-

---

[13] John O'Brien, "Ecclesiology as Narrative," *Ecclesiology* 4, no. 2 (2008): 150.

[14] Pius XI, *Mortalium Animos*, 10. This text can be accessed online at: http://www.vatican.va/holy_father/pius_xi/encyclicals/documents/hf_p-xi_enc _19280106_mortalium-animos_en.html.

tion of bishops to the conciliar commissions, successors to the preparatory commissions. This was to be conducted under the presidency of Cardinal Eugène Tisserant—a formidable, conservative curialist. A list of those bishops who served on the preparatory commissions was distributed among the council members with the clear expectation that these bishops would be reelected to the respective commissions. Had this occurred, it is difficult to know what course the council might have taken. But almost immediately following the distribution of the list, Cardinal Achille Liénart of Lille rose to speak. He moved that the election be postponed until the bishops could meet in regional caucuses in order to add their own nominations to the list of candidates. Cardinal Josef Frings of Cologne then stood up and seconded the motion. Almost immediately the motion was met with an ovation from the assembly and the first session was adjourned after only fifteen minutes! In that brief encounter, it became clear that this was not going to be a council content to rubber-stamp curial documents.

Montini's Plan for the Council

During the first week of the council Cardinal Giovanni Battista Montini of Milan (later Pope Paul VI) was beginning to panic that there was still no public plan for the council. He wrote a letter to Cardinal Cicognani—the content of which he was confident would be relayed to the pope—that expressed his concern. In essence he was asking why the Suenens plan was not being announced. Soon after, with Pope John's approval, Montini began to rework Suenens's plan. He mapped out a detailed agenda for the council, one that he envisioned would consist of three sessions (a fourth would eventually be necessary): the first being more doctrinal in character, the last two more pastoral. The pope was surprised at the mention of more than one session. He had only discovered that he had cancer in late September, and he desperately hoped to see the council through, assuming that it would be limited to one session. Nevertheless, he accepted the plan.

Removal of the Preparatory Schema on Divine Revelation

The next key event in redirecting the course of the council came immediately after the beginning of debate on the schema on divine revelation. Professors on the more conservative Lateran faculty had been the primary drafters of the document. A number of bishops rose to speak in opposition to the draft, most notably Cardinals Liénart, Frings, Léger, Bernard Alfrink (Utrecht), Suenens, Joseph Ritter (St. Louis), and Augustine Bea, president of the Secretariat for Promoting Christian Unity. The Italians, Ottaviani, Ernesto Ruffini (Palermo), and Giuseppe Siri (Genoa) all defended the draft. The major point of contention regarded the total disregard of modern biblical scholarship and the prominent place given to the so-called "two-source theory" of revelation. Liénart was adamant in his insistence on the rejection of this schema. He pointed out that the church had never formally taught that there were two sources of revelation but rather one font, the Word of God, transmitted in different modes.

After some time Ottaviani took a different procedural tack and claimed that the council rules did not permit the complete rejection of a schema but only its modification. Finally the secretary general, Archbishop Pericle Felici, called for a straw vote on the status of the schema. The explanation of the balloting offered by Cardinal Ruffini, however, was confusing, and it is apparent that not a few council members were unsure as to the implications of their vote. Nevertheless, 1,368 voted to reject the schema, 822 for retaining it. Since the rules required a 2/3 majority, the schema was narrowly retained. The next morning, however, Pope John ordered, on his own authority, that the schema be withdrawn and turned the matter over to a joint commission to be presided over by both Cardinals Ottaviani and Bea. The pope indicated that the new schema was to be short, irenic, and pastoral.

Domus Mariae

Recent scholarship has called attention to the role played by a group of bishops who were identified by the hotel in which they would meet regularly at the council, the *Domus Mariae*.[15] This group consisted of only twenty-two bishops, but they were all generally committed to the cause of conciliar reform. They met weekly to

---

[15] Melissa J. Wilde, *Vatican II: A Sociological Analysis of Religious Change* (Princeton, NJ: Princeton University Press, 2007).

discuss topics being considered by the council. Melissa Wilde notes that what was most significant about this small group was their organizational structure. They sought out bishops who were connected to the various national episcopal conferences. This allowed the *Domus Mariae* (DM) group to serve as a sort of clearing house for ideas. They would debate issues and offer compromise proposals that would then be disseminated to the bishops of the various conferences. This process accomplished several things. First, it provided a freer form of communal deliberation than was possible inside the council aula where bishops had to sign up often days or even weeks in advance to address the council and then only in Latin. Second, their methodology allowed for the rapid dissemination of ideas and a forum for individual episcopal conferences to raise their concerns.

Wilde compares the methodology employed by DM to that of a group of more traditionalist bishops led by Archbishop Marcel Lefebvre known as the *Coetus Internationalis Patrum* (CIP). This group included about sixteen bishops who were regularly active. The difference between these two groups represented a veritable clash of two cultures. On the one hand, the DM was very open to the emerging council discussion on episcopal collegiality. This gave them a practical advantage because it meant that they were comfortable making considerable use of the regional episcopal gatherings that were occurring informally during the council. On the other hand, the CIP, in no small part because of their distaste for the theological notion of episcopal collegiality, was much less inclined to use the episcopal conferences to their advantage. When there was a controversial measure or decision upcoming, the DM could mobilize bishops from all of the regional episcopal groupings and get word out to well over a thousand bishops in very little time. The CIP would contact known sympathizers, inevitably a much smaller group of bishops.

The Broadening of Episcopal Horizons

Yet another factor in redirecting the course was the broadening of episcopal horizons. We can begin with something as basic as the fact that the bishops were not allowed to sit by region, where they would have known those around them, but instead were seated by seniority based on their episcopal consecration. This created the circumstances in which an Italian bishop, for example, might sit next to a bishop from Africa. This seating arrangement encouraged a more wide-ranging exchange of diverse pastoral experiences and insights.

The opportunities for episcopal interaction also included provisions made for the bishops' refreshment while the council was in session. Bishops who struggled to stay awake during one mind-numbing Latin speech after another or who needed to smoke a cigarette often found respite at one of the coffee bars placed behind the bleachers (dubbed, tongue-in-cheek, "Bar-Abbas" and "Bar-Jonah"). There they often engaged in frank conversation on a variety of topics. Indeed one Australian prelate, Bishop John O'Loughlin from Darwin, penned the following limerick:

> We are two thousand padres in session,
> Who feel a great weight of oppression,
> What with cardinals talking,
> and lesser lights squawking,
> thank God the bar's so refreshing![16]

It was this kind of sustained, face-to-face conversation and the sharing of diverse experiences that opened episcopal eyes to new perspectives on the issues being deliberated.

It was no less true then than it is today that bishops often found it difficult to keep up with contemporary theological developments. Fortunately, many of the bishops realized their inadequate preparation for debate on the important issues before them. They soon turned to the many world-class theologians gathered in Rome for the council. National groups of bishops would often seek out the assistance of influential theologians. Yves Congar recounts time and again the tremendous burden he experienced in being called on so frequently to give presentations to various groups of bishops on a wide range of topics.[17] The bishops in attendance at the council

---

[16] Quoted in Ormond Rush, "The Australian Bishops of Vatican II: Participation and Reception," in *Vatican II: The Reception and Implementation in the Australian Church*, ed. Neil Ormerod, Ormond Rush, et al. (Melbourne: John Garrett, 2012), 4–19, at 10.

[17] This is a consistent theme in Congar's *My Journal of the Council* (Collegeville, MN: Liturgical Press, 2012).

would also attend evening lectures by such eminent scholars as Karl Rahner, Piet Fransen, and Barnabus Ahern. So threatening was the influence of these theologians that there were rumors Cardinal Ottaviani had petitioned John XXIII to have the Jesuit faculty members of the Pontifical Biblical Institute prohibited from giving lectures and to have Karl Rahner expelled from Rome.[18]

The well-known Vaticanologist Giancarlo Zizola tells the story of visiting Bishop Albino Luciani (the future Pope John Paul I) at a Roman *pensione* run by some Italian sisters. Luciani admitted that he tried to spend each afternoon in his room studying, because, as he put it:

> Everything I learned at the Gregorian is useless now. I have to become a student again. Fortunately I have an African bishop as a neighbor in the bleachers in the council hall, who gives me the texts of the experts of the German bishops. That way I can better prepare myself.[19]

Finally we must consider the influence of the daily celebration of the liturgy on the bishops gathered at the council. Often it was the practical experience of diversity that did more than anything else to move the bishops. All of the bishops celebrated the liturgy daily in St. Peter's Basilica, rotating the celebration of the different liturgical rites. For many of the bishops, this was their first exposure to the already existing diversity of liturgical rites in the church. This experience helped them appreciate the church universal as more than a corporation of branch offices of the Roman church; it included all the many Eastern churches as well. On November 28, 1962, Archbishop Yemmeru Asrate of Addis Ababa celebrated, with the entire assembly, the Ethiopian liturgy. Here is Xavier Rynne's account:

> The rite itself was extremely ancient, going back in outline at least to the fourth century, but with many later additions and ceremonies of a distinctly African flavor. It was characterized by moving simplicity and solemnity. The language was classical Ethiopian or Gheez. As the book of Gospels was being enthroned, the spirited chanting of the

[18] Xavier Rynne, *Vatican Council II* (New York: Farrar, Straus & Giroux, 1968), 92.

[19] Giancarlo Zizola, "He Answered Papal Summons to Journalism," *National Catholic Reporter* (October 4, 2002): 10.

seminarians and priests belonging to the Ethiopian College on Vatican Hill behind St. Peter's—they also chanted the mass—was accompanied by the deep rhythms of African drums, the ringing of bells, and the shaking of tambourines, causing the New York *Journal American* to headline its story: "African drums boom in Vatican rite."[20]

All of these factors, taken together, created a new ecclesial dynamic at the council, one that was able to overcome the severe handicaps imposed on the bishops at the outset.

III. What Can We Learn from the Forces That Redirected the Course of the Council?

In the chapters that follow we will have ample opportunity to reflect on the enduring significance of conciliar teaching. But, at the end of this narrative of the council that should have failed but didn't, it is worth asking what we can learn, not from the council's teaching but from the conciliar dynamics recounted above.

First, we must attend to the quite different conceptions of church leadership represented by Pope John and many members of the Roman Curia. The key point of difference was not, as one might expect, doctrinal or even ideological. There is no evidence from Pope John's past that he aligned himself with the more progressive voices in the church such as that of the Swiss theologian Hans Küng. Pope John's leadership was marked by a more historical and pastoral vision of church doctrine, something he learned from his time as secretary to Bishop Giacomo Radini Tedeschi, that great preconciliar advocate of a more pastoral and socially engaged form of Catholicism.[21] Pope John had, over the course of his diverse ecclesiastical career, learned what might be gained by a careful reading of the signs of the times when combined with a confidence in the work of the Spirit in the church.

Many, but certainly not all, of the members of the Curia were more preoccupied with a form of church leadership characterized by "bureaucratic maintenance." They believed that those who were part

---

[20] Rynne, *Vatican Council II*, 104.

[21] Massimo Faggioli, *John XXIII: The Medicine of Mercy* (Collegeville, MN: Liturgical Press, 2014), 29–45.

of the institutional structures were best equipped to lead and direct any institutional reform. Moreover, they generally held that such reform should occur only in small, carefully calibrated increments. We can still see evidence of both conceptions of church leadership at work in the church today. Indeed, it is not a stretch to see Pope Francis reenacting this battle between two styles of leadership in his efforts to reform the Curia and to encourage a more dynamic and dialogical account of the church. We will return to the leadership of Pope Francis in the sixth chapter.

A second ecclesial dynamic at work at the council could be described as *the catholicity of dialogue*. Here I am using the term *catholic* in keeping with its etymological roots. *Katholikos* is derived from the Greek root *kat'holou*, "pertaining to or oriented toward the whole." Catholicity affirms the fundamental unity-in-diversity of the church. Ecclesial dialogue is *catholic* to the extent that it freely engages different perspectives and insights. During the four conciliar sessions, bishops were introduced to other bishops from other countries and continents—bishops who looked at key pastoral and theological issues from strikingly different perspectives. They met with theologians, ecumenical observers, and lay auditors, men and women,[22] all of whom helped to broaden their perspectives on the issues at hand.

The catholicity of dialogue evident at the council shines a harsh light on the situation of our church today. We seek to live out our faith in a culture that has become increasingly uncivil. Today we encounter toxic, demonizing rhetoric on cable television, talk radio, and the blogosphere. Yet the council reminds us of the Christian obligation to respectful conversation with people whose views may differ markedly from our own. The conduct of the council teaches us that a precondition for the possibility of genuine ecclesial discernment is the conviction that none of us individually has all the answers. We discover the guidance of the Spirit and we penetrate the power and significance of God's Word through ecclesial conversation and the

---

[22] For more on the underappreciated role of the women auditors, see Carmel McEnroy, *Guests in Their Own House: The Women of Vatican II* (New York: Crossroad, 1996; reprint ed., Eugene, OR: Wipf and Stock, 2011); Catherine Clifford, *Decoding Vatican II: Interpretation and Ongoing Reception* (New York: Paulist Press, 2014), 66–72.

opportunity to interact with believers who offer us different insights, experiences, and questions.

A third dynamic of the council was the bishops' commitment to *humble learning*. In the century prior to the council, it had become common to divide the church into two parts: a teaching church (*ecclesia docens*) comprised of the clergy and a learning church (*ecclesia discens*) comprised of the laity. The hierocratic form of the church presumed that the bishops had a monopoly on divine truth. In fact, Catholic teaching is clear that bishops do not receive supernaturally infused knowledge at their episcopal ordination. It is not as if a priest who was a little shaky in his understanding of the relationship between the immanent and economic Trinity on the day before his episcopal ordination would suddenly be able to give learned lectures on the topic on the day after ordination! As St. Cyprian of Carthage sagely pointed out in the third century, bishops must themselves be learners before they can be teachers.

> But it is unrepentant presumption and insolence that induces men to defend their own perverse errors instead of giving assent to what is right and true, but has come from another. . . . It is thus a bishop's duty not only to teach but also to learn. For he becomes a better teacher if he makes daily progress and advancement in learning what is better.[23]

When the International Theological Commission (ITC) was created under Pope Paul VI, many hoped for new developments in theological consultation in which the pope, the various Vatican dicasteries, and all the bishops would consult internationally with respected theologians belonging to different schools of thought. The pope had envisioned that the commission would serve a consultative role not only to the pope himself but also to the Congregation for the Doctrine of the Faith (CDF). This important papal initiative must be expanded. A frequent consultation of theologians representing divergent views on a matter need not threaten the legitimate authority of those who hold church office.

Unfortunately, under the pontificates of John Paul II and Benedict XVI, the diversity of views represented by the ITC membership diminished considerably, and some fear a return to the practice of

[23] Cyprian of Carthage, *Epistle*, 74, 10.

limiting Vatican consultation to "court theologians." There has been no evidence, as of yet, that the ITC membership will be reconfigured under Pope Francis. On the current commission roster, only five of the thirty theologians are women and none are by training or ideological predilection likely to offer the many contributions of contemporary feminist theology to the commission's deliberations. Yet another proposed reform would demand revised structures for theological consultation at the local and universal levels. Here again, these structures must allow for legitimate and respectful dissent from authoritative, noninfallible teaching.

It is true that the church today has much to learn from the teaching of Vatican II, and we must continue to work toward the dissemination of the teaching of the council. What I have proposed in this chapter, however, is that we can also learn much from the *conduct* of the council. The council's conduct offers us a model for a church led by those who are willing to read the signs of the times and foster a genuine community of discernment. We are now in a position to shift from an exploration of the ecclesial dynamics at work at the council itself to a consideration of its fundamental contributions to the construction of a new form of the church adequate to the demands of our age.

3

Toward a New Ecclesial Form

The Pillars of Vatican II's Ecclesial Vision

We return again to the extended metaphor that has provided an architectonic structure for this volume, the rebuilding of a new "basilica" while the remnants of the old were left standing. In chapter 1, we explored the central features of the old "basilica," the hierocratic form of the church. In the last chapter we considered the story of the council from the perspective of the conciliar dynamics that enabled the council bishops to sketch out the beginnings of an alternative form of the church, one more capable of responding to the needs of the age. In this chapter we will outline seven "pillars" or distinct conciliar contributions that provide the foundations for this new ecclesial form. Chapters 4 and 5 will then propose two complementary ways of drawing these pillars together into a coherent, integrated ecclesial vision, one that can underwrite the kind of substantive ecclesial reform that Pope Francis is offering the church today.

I. Kerygmatic and Trinitarian Theology of Divine Revelation

In the last ten years, a growing number of theologians have emphasized the interpretive priority of Vatican II's *Dei Verbum* (The Dogmatic Constitution on Divine Revelation) and its theology of revelation.[1] In *Dei Verbum*, we recognize a move away from the propositional theology of revelation that was central to the hierocratic form of the church. The council instead returned to a more ancient theology of divine revelation, one that begins with a trinitarian account of God revealing God's self to us in Christ by the power of the Holy Spirit.

> It pleased God, in his goodness and wisdom, to reveal himself and to make known the mystery of his will, which was that people can draw near to the Father, through Christ, the Word made flesh, in the holy Spirit, and thus become sharers in the divine nature. (DV 2)

The council's theology of revelation is kerygmatic in its orientation toward the fundamental Christian message. In this regard, the council's theology of revelation is also deeply christocentric; it begins not with doctrines but with Christ and God's desire that we enter into a communion of divine friendship through Christ and in the Spirit.

> By this revelation, then, the invisible God, from the fullness of his love, addresses men and women as his friends, and lives among them in order to invite and receive them into his own company. (DV 2)

The council offers an account of revelation that gives priority to spiritual communion with God. What God shares with us is the divine self encountered in spiritual friendship. The "knowledge" we acquire through this revelation is, in the first instance, the kind of knowledge gained in personal relationship. It is not, in other words, like the knowledge of chemistry obtained through the periodic table or the knowledge one might acquire through consulting a train schedule.

The propositional theology of revelation also presented revelation as an event of divine communication, but it imagined that communication as unidirectional, coming from God through Scripture, tradition, and the magisterium to the church. *Dei Verbum*, by contrast,

---

[1] See, especially, Christoph Theobald, *"Dans les traces . . ." de la constitution "Dei Verbum" du concile Vatican II. Bible, théologie et pratiques de lecture* (Paris: Cerf, 2009); Theobald, *La réception du concile Vatican II: Accéder à la source*, vol. 1 (Paris: Cerf, 2009); Ormond Rush, *Still Interpreting Vatican II: Some Hermeneutical Principles* (Mahwah, NJ: Paulist Press, 2004); Jared Wicks, "Vatican II on Revelation—From Behind the Scenes," *Theological Studies* 71 (2010): 637–50.

sees this event of divine communication as genuinely dialogical; God's self-communication invites, even demands, our response as a response of faith and communion.[2]

> For this faith to be accorded we need the grace of God, anticipating it and assisting it, as well as the interior helps of the holy Spirit, who moves the heart and converts it to God, and opens the eyes of the mind and "makes it easy for all to accept and believe the truth." (DV 5)

This shift has significant implications for the life of the church. Within the propositional theology of revelation, normative teaching and docile obedience were primary. If, however, the revelatory event is truly dialogical, then church teaching can no longer be strictly discursive in character; we must conceive of the whole church, including those who hold episcopal office, as participating in the church's teaching *and learning*. The council stressed this at numerous points.

First, it recognized the need for theological and biblical scholarship to assist the church in the discovery of God's Word. The tools of modern biblical scholarship are necessary in order to arrive at an adequate interpretation and reception of the Word of God as it is mediated through Scripture (DV 12). Theology must interpret divine revelation in the light of a considered engagement with modern research in the sciences (GS 62). Second, it resituated the authority of the magisterium:

> This magisterium is not superior to the word of God, but is rather its servant. It teaches only what has been handed on to it. At the divine command and with the help of the holy Spirit, it listens to this devoutly, guards it reverently and expounds it faithfully. All that it proposes for belief as being divinely revealed it draws from this sole deposit of faith. (DV 10)

This passage invites the question, if the magisterium teaches only what has been handed on to it, the fruit of its devout listening, then how is that word handed on to it and to whom does it listen? The answer would include, of course, Scripture and tradition that together

---

[2] For a development of the communicative nature of God and divine revelation, see Matthias Scharer and Bernd Jochen Hilberath, *The Practice of Communicative Theology* (New York: Crossroad, 2008), 64–79.

comprise the one deposit of faith. But insofar as that tradition is a living tradition, it grows, develops, and is handed on at least in part through the experience and witness of ordinary believers (DV 8). The contributions of ordinary believers to the development of tradition and its transmission from generation to generation and church to church are only possible because, according to the council, all baptized believers possess a supernatural instinct for the faith (*sensus fidei*) that allows them to acquire a deeper penetration of the meaning of God's Word.

I have contended that it was the intention of the council to move away from a strictly propositional theology of revelation. That does not mean, however, that the council wished to reject the necessity and value of propositional truths.[3] It is true that the council offered no systematic consideration of the role of dogma and doctrine within this more kerygmatic and trinitarian theology of revelation. The council did, however, provide several suggestive indications of what such a reconceived role might be. First, the council affirmed the historical embeddedness of church doctrine. Doctrine is never encountered in some hermetically sealed container. It emerges out of particular historical, cultural, and pastoral contexts and it is always interpreted within particular historical, cultural, and pastoral contexts. Consequently, it is incumbent on theologians to find new ways of "communicating doctrine to the people of today for the deposit and the truths of faith are one thing, the manner of expressing them—provided their sense and meaning are retained—is quite another" (GS 62). This distinction between the substance and the specific formulation of doctrine represents an acknowledgment that doctrine is always historically conditioned. Consequently, the interpretation of church doctrine requires knowledge of the specific historical contexts in which it was first formulated and in which it is being appropriated. This is implicitly acknowledged in *Optatam Totius* (The Decree on the Training of Priests), which stressed a much more historically informed study of church doctrine, one that should observe the following order:

---

[3] Some interpretations of the council's theology of revelation have, in my view, gone too far in their characterization of this shift, to the point of virtually dismissing the normative value of propositional teaching. See John Haught, *The Revelation of God in History* (Wilmington, DE: Michael Glazier, 1988).

Let biblical themes be treated first, then what the Fathers of the church
(both east and west) have contributed to the faithful transmission and
explanation of revealed truths, followed by the later history of dogma,
including its relation to the general history of the church. (OT 16)

Another example of the council's reconceived understanding of
doctrine is found in *Unitatis Redintegratio* (The Decree on Ecumenism). There, in the context of the obligations that obtain for theologians engaged in ecumenical dialogue, the council writes: "When
comparing doctrines with one another, they should remember that
in catholic doctrine there exists an order or 'hierarchy' of truths,
since they vary in their relation to the foundation of the Christian
faith" (UR 11). In this brief passage, the council introduced a crucial
distinction between the substance of divine revelation ("foundation
of the Christian faith"), understood as God's self-communication in
Christ by the power of the Spirit, and those church doctrines that, in
varying degrees, *symbolically mediate* that revelation. Moreover, the
council seemed to suggest, as well, that the content of some doctrinal
truths was closer to the kerygmatic foundation of faith (e.g., Trinity,
Christ) than others (e.g., the immaculate conception).

When the council first articulated this teaching in *Unitatis Redintegratio*, Oscar Cullmann, noted Protestant theologian and observer
at the council, remarked that this teaching was "the most revolu-
tionary . . . not only in the schema *De Oecumenismo*, but in all
the schemas of the council."[4] This text offers an account of doctrine
that avoids the propositional model's tendency to reduce revelation
to its propositional expression. In the Decree on Ecumenism, the
council appreciates the role of doctrine in symbolically mediating a
reality that is, nevertheless, more "foundational" than the doctrinal
expressions themselves.[5]

---

[4] Oscar Cullman, "Comments on the Decree on Ecumenism," *Ecumenical
Review* 17 (1965): 93.

[5] The symbolic mediation of revelation by way of doctrine is productively
explored in Avery Dulles, *Models of Revelation* (New York: Doubleday, 1983),
especially 131–73; and Gerard O'Collins, *Rethinking Fundamental Theology:
Toward a New Fundamental Theology* (Oxford: Oxford University Press, 2011),
especially 37–87.

II. Dialogical Engagement

A second pillar in the council's efforts to construct a new theological vision for the church concerns the council's commitment to the ecclesial habit of dialogical engagement. According to the church historian John O'Malley, one of the most striking features of the council was its emphasis on the priority of dialogue.[6] As we saw in chapter 2, Pope John spoke of the need for an ecclesial shift from condemnation to persuasion. This commitment to a dialogical understanding of the church was further emphasized by Pope John's successor, Pope Paul VI, whose first encyclical, *Ecclesiam Suam*, promulgated while the council was still in session, was dedicated to the priority of dialogue for the life of the church and its engagement with other Christians, adherents of other world religions, and the world itself.

Following the lead of both conciliar popes, the council bishops highlighted, in a number of key texts, the dialogical character of ecclesial life. In *Gaudium et Spes* (The Pastoral Constitution on the Church in the Modern World Today), the bishops acknowledge that there will often be disagreements among Christians regarding how, concretely, they should best apply their faith to the pressing challenges they face in their daily lives. The social questions they will face are often quite complex, and the bishops were realistic about the difficulties involved with this task.

> Very often their Christian vision will suggest a certain solution in some given situation. Yet it happens rather frequently, and legitimately so, that some of the faithful, with no less sincerity, will see the problem quite differently. (GS 43)

Christians must resist the temptation to identify their own position too easily with the Gospel itself. The bishops encourage Christians in such a conflict situation: "Let them, then, try to guide each other by sincere dialogue in a spirit of mutual charity and with a genuine concern for the common good above all" (GS 43). Local parishes pro-

---

[6] This is a reoccurring theme in John W. O'Malley, *What Happened at Vatican II* (Cambridge, MA: Harvard University Press, 2008).

vide, the council bishops contend, a natural context for this ecclesial dialogue.

> The laity should develop the habit of working in the parish in close cooperation with their priests, of bringing before the ecclesial community their own problems, world problems, and questions regarding humanity's salvation, to examine them together and solve them by general discussion. (AA 10)

For the council bishops, this commitment to dialogue within the church is put to the service of the church's mission.

> Such a mission requires us first of all to create in the church itself mutual esteem, reverence and harmony, and to acknowledge all legitimate diversity; in this way all who constitute the one people of God will be able to engage in ever more fruitful dialogue, whether they are pastors or other members of the faithful. For the ties which unite the faithful together are stronger than those which separate them: let there be unity in what is necessary, freedom in what is doubtful, and charity in everything. (GS 92)

These passages offer a surprisingly realistic account of ecclesial dialogue, one that recognizes the reality of conflict and disagreement and which understands that being in complete agreement on all matters is not necessary for Christian unity or to share in the church's mission in the world.

The council's commitment to dialogical engagement informed its consideration of pastoral leadership as well. No longer were ordinary Christians exhorted to a docile and unthinking obedience to their pastors. Clergy and professed religious, "in constant dialogue with the laity," are to make "painstaking search for methods capable of making apostolic action more fruitful" (AA 25). The relationship between the laity and their pastors needs to be established on the grounds of mutual respect:

> The laity should disclose their needs and desires to the pastors with that liberty and confidence which befits children of God and brothers and sisters in Christ. To the extent of their knowledge, competence or authority the laity are entitled, and indeed sometimes duty-bound, to express their opinion on matters which concern the good of the church. (LG 37)

Presbyterorum Ordinis (The Decree on Priestly Ministry and Life) begins its reflection on the relationship between priests and the laity with a reminder that priests stand among the laity as brothers since they all share a common baptism. "They should be willing to listen to lay people, give brotherly consideration to their wishes, and recognize their experience and competence in the different fields of human activity" (PO 9).

This spirit of dialogue between pastors and the laity is applied as well to the relationships between a bishop and his priests: "[Bishops] should be glad to listen to their priests' views and to consult them and hold conference with them about matters that concern the needs of pastoral work and the good of the diocese" (PO 7).

The council would extend this commitment to dialogue beyond the Roman Catholic Church to its engagements with non-Catholic Christians. In *Unitatis Redintegratio* the council effectively repudiated a preconciliar "ecumenism of return" in favor of an honest dialogue with other Christians in which Catholicism would have to admit that in past divisions within the body of Christ, "people on both sides were to blame" (UR 3). The council bishops offered some basic habits of ecumenical dialogue. For example, the bishops insist that every effort must be made to avoid unfair representations of the positions of one's dialogue partner. This dialogue must be undertaken in a spirit of prayer and mutual respect. Each dialogue partner must be willing to "examine their own faithfulness to Christ's will for the church and, wherever necessary, undertake with vigor the task of renewal and reform" (UR 4). In this regard, the primary duty of Catholics is

> to make a careful and honest appraisal of whatever needs to be renewed and done in the Catholic household itself, in order that its life may bear witness more clearly and more faithfully to the teachings and institutions which have been handed down by Christ through the apostles. (UR 4)

This dialogue must be marked by a determination to "acknowledge and esteem" what we share in common with our dialogue partners (UR 4). It must avoid a false irenicism and be mindful of the hierarchy of truths when attending to doctrinal differences (UR 11).

The commitment to dialogical engagement was extended even further to the church's relationship to other world religions. In *Nos-*

tra Aetate (The Declaration on the Relation of the Church to Non-Christian Religions), the church

> urges its sons and daughters to enter with prudence and charity into discussion and collaboration with members of other religions. Let Christians, while witnessing to their own faith and way of life, acknowledge, preserve and encourage the spiritual and moral truths found among non-Christians, together with their social life and culture. (NA 2)

Finally, in *Gaudium et Spes*, the council recognized a properly dialogical relationship with the world itself. Within that dialogical relationship the church has much to offer the world. First and foremost, it brings to the world its most precious gift, the Good News of Jesus Christ and the proclamation of his coming reign (GS 41–43). At the same time

> the church is not unaware how much it has profited from the history and development of humankind. It profits from the experience of past ages, from the progress of the sciences, and from the riches hidden in various cultures, through which greater light is thrown on human nature and new avenues to truth are opened up. (GS 44)

Many more passages could be marshaled in support of this theme, but this brief summary should suffice to demonstrate the significant contribution of this second pillar in conciliar teaching.

III. The Priority of Baptism

We discussed in chapter 1 the place of a sacral priesthood in the hierocratic form of the church. The sacral priesthood created a gaping ontological divide between the clergy and the laity. It encouraged Pope Pius X's characterization of the church as a *societas inequalis*, an unequal society comprised of two ranks, clergy and laity. This conception of the church actually had roots going back to the teaching of the canonist Gratian in the twelfth century who said quite simply that there were two kind of Christians, lay and cleric. The council directly challenged this conception of the church.

It is tempting to see the council's constructive, positive theology of the laity as its most direct antidote to the sacral priesthood and the ecclesial acids of clericalism. The council's more fundamental response, however, lay in its reaffirmation of the priority of Christian baptism. In a number of texts the council reminded us that it was baptism and not ordination or marriage or professed vows that confers our most basic Christian identity. *Sacrosanctum Concilium* (The Constitution on the Sacred Liturgy) reminded us not only in its call for the reform of the rites of initiation but also in its focus on the whole worshipping assembly that our primary identity as Christians is not as lay or cleric but as members of the baptized called to participate in the life and worship of the church.

> It is very much the wish of the church that all the faithful should be led to take that full, conscious, and active part in liturgical celebrations which is demanded by the very nature of the liturgy, and to which the Christian people, "a chosen race, a royal priesthood, a holy nation, a redeemed people," have a right and to which they are bound by reasons of their Baptism. (SC 14)

Note that this passage is not referring to the participation of the laity but to "all the faithful." Christ acts in the liturgy by the power of the Holy Spirit through the entire gathered assembly, priest and people.

Sacrosanctum Concilium also introduced, if indirectly, Catholicism's recovery of a theology of the baptismal priesthood. This teaching had been avoided in Catholic thought ever since the Reformation when Martin Luther had placed the biblical teaching on the priesthood of the baptized in opposition to a sacramentally ordained ministerial priesthood. Article 7 of *Sacrosanctum Concilium* taught that the entire liturgy was itself an action of the priestly ministry of Christ. The ministerial priest participates in Christ's own priesthood in his presidency over the church's eucharistic liturgy just as all the faithful share in their own way in that priestly ministry, "offering the immaculate victim, not only through the hands of the priest but also together with him" (SC 48). The priesthood of the baptized would be further developed in *Lumen Gentium.*

> The baptized, by regeneration and the anointing of the holy Spirit, are consecrated as a spiritual house and a holy priesthood, that through all their Christian activities they may offer spiritual sacrifices and proclaim the marvels of him who has called them out of darkness into his wonderful light. (LG 10)

The council bishops entertained numerous proposals that would have treated the priesthood of the baptized as a lesser priesthood, a priesthood in only an inchoate or analogous sense.[7] The bishops rejected these, however, teaching instead that although the ministerial priesthood and the baptismal priesthood "differ essentially and not only in degree, the common priesthood of the faithful and the ministerial or hierarchical priesthood are none the less interrelated; each in its own way shares in the one priesthood of Christ" (LG 10).

The council's commitment to the priority of baptism was further in evidence in structural changes that were made to earlier drafts of *Lumen Gentium*. The decision to place the chapter on the people of God before the chapter on the hierarchy[8] expressed a profound ecclesiological principle: we must begin with what unites us—faith and baptism—before we can consider what distinguishes us (e.g., ordination). Later the council would quote from St. Augustine's Sermon 340:

> When I am frightened by what I am to you, then I am consoled by what I am with you. To you I am the bishop, with you I am a Christian. The first is an office, the second a grace; the first a danger, the second salvation. (LG 32)

Giving priority to our baptismal identity does not negate, of course, the fact that Christians may be further "ordered" in service of the church by sacramental ordination. It does mean, as Bishop Franjo Seper of Zagreb noted at the council, that the ordained do not cease being members of the people of God after ordination; the obligations that are theirs by virtue of baptism and confirmation still remain.[9]

The practical import of this recovery of the priority of our baptismal identity is pithily summed up in the off-handed remark of one of

---

[7] Melvin Michalski, *The Relationship between the Universal Priesthood of the Baptized and the Ministerial Priesthood of the Ordained in Vatican II and in Subsequent Theology* (Lewiston, NY: Mellen University Press, 1996), 40–41.

[8] For the history of the key changes that occurred in the drafting of *Lumen Gentium*, see Richard R. Gaillardetz, *The Church in the Making:* Lumen Gentium, Christus Dominus, Orientalium Ecclesiarum, Rediscovering Vatican II Series (New York: Paulist Press, 2006), 8–27.

[9] *Acta Synodalia* 2/3, 202.

the most influential bishops at the council, Belgium's Cardinal Leo Suenens: "The greatest day in the life of the pope is not that of his election or coronation, but the day on which he receives that which the Greek fathers call the holy and unbreakable seal of baptismal regeneration."[10]

IV. Renewed Theology of the Holy Spirit

In continuity with the teaching of Pius XII, the council offered a beautiful meditation on the church as the Body of Christ, but it added to this an equally profound reflection on the role of the Holy Spirit in the life of the church. Vatican II took decisive steps toward recovering the long neglected place of a theology of the Holy Spirit, or pneumatology, in Catholic ecclesiology.[11] Since no one deserves more credit for lifting up the importance of pneumatology at Vatican II than Yves Congar, an influential *peritus* at the council, we might consider his own description of pneumatology:

> By pneumatology, I mean something other than a simple dogmatic theology of the third Person. I also mean something more than, and in this sense different from, a profound analysis of the indwelling of the Holy Spirit in individual souls and his sanctifying activity there. Pneumatology should, I believe, describe the impact, in the context of a vision of the Church, of the fact that the Spirit distributes his gifts as he wills and in this way builds up the Church. A study of this kind involves not simply a consideration of those gifts or charisms, but a theology of the Church.[12]

[10] Cardinal Leó Suenens, *Co-Responsibility in the Church* (New York: Herder, 1968), 31.

[11] See André-Marie Charue, "Le Saint-Esprit dans '*Lumen Gentium*'," *Ephemerides theologicae lovanienses* 45 (1969): 358–79. Mary Cecily Boulding, "The Doctrine of the Holy Spirit in the Documents of Vatican II," *Irish Theological Quarterly* 51 (1985): 253–67; Sally Vance-Trembath, *The Pneumatology of Vatican II: With Particular Reference to* Lumen Gentium *and* Gaudium et Spes (Saarbrücken, Germany: Lambert Academic Publishing, 2009).

[12] Yves Congar, "The Place of the Holy Spirit in Catholicism Since the Counter-Reformation," in *I Believe in the Holy Spirit* (New York: Seabury, 1983), 1:151–59, at 156.

We can locate the beginning of the council's recovery of pneumatology with Pope John XXIII who, from the preparatory period all the way to his address at the close of the first session of the council, would express the hope on numerous occasions that the council might become a "new Pentecost."[13] This allusion to Pentecost is decisive for grasping the council's pneumatology. After Christ's death and resurrection, the Holy Spirit came down upon the believers gathered in Jerusalem. As those who received the Holy Spirit gave testimony to God's deeds, Jewish foreigners from throughout the known world all heard and comprehended their testimonies. The Spirit, allowing each to understand the other, transcended linguistic differences. In the account of Pentecost found in Acts 2, those diaspora Jews who had gathered in Jerusalem from other lands heard those giving witness *in their own languages*. Cultural difference was not destroyed but became the very instrument for a realization of a more profound unity-in-difference. John XXIII's repeated allusions to Pentecost, allusions that would be taken up by many commentators on the work of the council,[14] suggest that the entire sphere of conciliar action can be read within the framework of Pentecost, a dramatic outpouring of the Spirit.

As Congar wrote in an essay published late in his career, it would not be correct to attribute to the council a fully developed pneumatology in spite of the 258 different references to the Holy Spirit in the council documents.[15] Nevertheless, what the council did offer was considerable. In the very first chapter of *Lumen Gentium*, it teaches that it is the Holy Spirit "which dwells in the church and in the hearts of the faithful as in a temple" (LG 4). *Lumen Gentium* attributes to both Christ and the Spirit a role in the establishment of the church: "Christ when he was lifted up from the earth drew all humanity to himself. Rising from the dead he sent his life-giving spirit upon his disciples and through him set up his body which is the

---

[13] For an extended treatment on the ubiquity of this biblical image in the many addresses of John XXIII, see Thomas Hughson, "Interpreting Vatican II: A New Pentecost," *Theological Studies* 69 (2008): 3–37.

[14] None more famously than Cardinal Leo Suenens in his book, *A New Pentecost?* (New York: Seabury, 1975).

[15] Yves Congar, "The Pneumatology of Vatican II," in *I Believe in the Holy Spirit*, 1:167–73, at 167.

church as the universal sacrament of salvation" (LG 48). The council presents the Spirit as the principle of growth and development within the life of the church. The interrelated missions of Word and Spirit flow from God's initiative. In *Lumen Gentium* the council quotes St. Cyprian, declaring, "the Church has been seen as 'a people made one with the unity of the Father, the Son and the Holy Spirit'" (LG 4). *Sacrosanctum Concilium* describes the church's sacramental life as a trinitarian participation in the paschal mystery:

> Thus by baptism men and women are implanted into the paschal mystery of Christ; they die with him, are buried with Him, and rise with him. They receive the spirit of adoption as sons and daughters "in which we cry: Abba, Father," and thus become true adorers such as the Father seeks. (SC 6)

The council's recovery of a theology of the Holy Spirit is evident in two particularly significant conciliar contributions: its theology of charisms and its theology of the sense of the faithful.

The council taught that the Spirit "guides the church in the way of all truth and, uniting it in fellowship and ministry, bestows upon it different hierarchic and charismatic gifts, and in this way directs it and adorns it with his fruits" (LG 4). By appealing to the biblical concept of charism, the council acknowledged the indispensable role of all the faithful in building up the church and assisting in the fulfillment of the church's mission in the world. The bishops wrote: "It is not only through the sacraments and the ministries that the holy Spirit makes the people holy, leads them and enriches them with his virtues. Allotting his gifts 'at will to each individual,' he also distributes special graces among the faithful of every rank" (LG 12). Although few if any at the council could have anticipated the flourishing of lay ministries that would occur in the ensuing decades, it is this emphasis on the charisms of all the baptized that provided a helpful theological framework for interpreting that later postconciliar development of lay ministry.

The second fruit of the council's renewed pneumatology is its teaching that the whole Christian faithful, "from the bishops down to the last of the lay faithful," share in a "supernatural discernment in matters of faith." This spiritual gift is often referred to by the Latin term, *sensus fidei*. The people of God "adheres unwaveringly to the faith given once and for all to the saints, penetrates it more deeply with right thinking, and applies it more fully in its life" (LG 12, see also LG 35). It is this capacity that allows a believer, almost intuitively, to sense what is of God and what is not. As we saw earlier, the council's teaching on the sense of faith contributes to its dialogical understanding of revelation in which all God's people play a necessary role in "hearing the Word of God."

V. Episcopal Collegiality

The council's teaching on episcopal collegiality offers yet another pillar in its unfinished project. The council distanced itself from almost a thousand years of papal monarchialism. It was a project the need for which had been acknowledged almost immediately after the suspension of Vatican I. The eminent English theologian John Henry Newman had vigorously defended that council's teaching on the papacy even as he was prescient in his prediction that it would be widely misunderstood. Newman recognized the danger of the one-sided papo-centrism likely to follow Vatican I's definition on papal infallibility.

> The late definition [on papal infallibility] does not so much need to be undone, as to be completed. It needs *safeguards* to the Pope's possible acts—explanations as to the matter and extent of his power. I know that a violent reckless party, had it its will, would at this moment define that the Pope's power needs no safeguards, no explanations; but there is a limit to the triumph of the tyrannical. Let us be patient, let us have faith, and a new Pope, and a re-assembled Council may trim the boat.[16]

The council did indeed seek to "trim the boat," largely by way of the cautious exposition of the doctrine of episcopal collegiality. Although the council was careful to reaffirm Vatican I's teaching on papal primacy and papal infallibility, it reached back to a more ancient tradition, recalling the bond of communion shared both among the

---

[16] John Henry Newman, *The Letters and Diaries of John Henry Newman*, ed. Charles Stephen Dessain and Thomas Gornall (Oxford: Clarendon Press, 1973), 27:310. The emphasis is Newman's.

bishops and between the bishops and the Bishop of Rome. The council recalled, for example, the ancient custom of bishops gathering to deliberate at synods and councils (LG 23). It insisted that although the college of bishops has no authority on its own apart from communion with its head the pope, the college shares with the Bishop of Rome, and never apart from him, "supreme and full power over the universal church" (LG 22).

This teaching was developed in the third chapter of *Lumen Gentium* and, to a lesser extent, in chapters 1 and 3 of *Christus Dominus* (The Decree on the Pastoral Office of the Bishop). It is a good example of conciliar teaching contributing to a substantive development in doctrine. The extent of this development, however, was limited by excessive caution. The flow of chapter 3 of *Lumen Gentium* is hobbled by a determination to anticipate and forestall at every turn the argument that the council's teaching on episcopal collegiality was a rejection of Vatican I.[17] Throughout that chapter we find repeated assurances of the unfettered authority of the pope over the college of bishops, passages clearly aimed at the nervous minority group of bishops concerned with episcopal collegiality. Adding to that caution was a controversial explanatory note attached to the third chapter at the eleventh hour by "higher authority" and without a council vote. This *nota praevia* gave a decidedly restricted, juridical interpretation to the council's teaching. This excessive caution may help explain why the council's proposals regarding concrete institutional expressions of the principle of collegiality were so underdeveloped.

A number of bishops had proposed that the council consider the creation of a permanent body of bishops that would share with the pope the ministry of universal pastoral leadership. The Eastern bishops offered their experience with permanent synods of bishops that shared deliberative authority with the metropolitan or patriarch. Unfortunately, these proposals were hamstrung by Pope Paul VI's unilateral decision to promulgate *Apostolica Solicitudo*, establishing a synod that was not permanent, possessed no deliberative authority, and which would meet only periodically. Fifty years later, it is

[17] Gérard Philips, "Dogmatic Constitution on the Church: History of the Constitution," in *Commentary on the Documents of Vatican II*, ed. Herbert Vorgrimler (New York: Crossroad, 1989), 1:129.

hard not to see the irony in a pope acting independently and without episcopal collaboration to create a structure intended to enhance episcopal collegiality.

The council bishops had firsthand experience of the value of meeting in regional groupings to deliberate on matters of shared concern. At several points, the bishops recommended greater development of episcopal conferences as an institutional instrument for manifesting episcopal collegiality. The council granted considerable authority to these conferences in the Constitution on the Sacred Liturgy (SC 22), and in *Christus Dominus* the bishops assert a connection between the role of episcopal conferences and the ancient tradition of regional bishops meeting in synods (CD 36). In spite of these promising forays, however, the council did not answer the difficult question regarding the extent to which synods and episcopal conferences participate in genuine collegial authority. This cautionary stance would hamper postconciliar efforts to develop more robust collegial structures.

VI. The Church Is by Its Nature Missionary

In the evolving field of Vatican II studies, we see an emerging consensus regarding the thoroughly missiological character of the council's teaching. This missiological emphasis is most explicit in *Gaudium et Spes* and *Ad Gentes*, yet Stephen Bevans has persuasively demonstrated that the theme is elaborated in virtually every council document and with particular force in the four constitutions.[18]

Consider the first document debated and promulgated at the council, *Sacrosanctum Concilium*. We can see the missionary thrust of the liturgical reform in the acceptance of the vernacular and the increased sensitivity to local cultures and customs (SC 37). When the council portrays the liturgy as "the summit toward which the activity of the church is directed; at the same time it is the fountain from which all her power flows" (SC 10), it is making, according to Bevans, a profound missionary statement. The liturgy is not to be

[18] Stephen B. Bevans, "Revisiting Mission at Vatican II: Theology and Practice for Today's Missionary Church," *Theological Studies* 74 (June 2013): 261–83.

a graced refuge from the world but a ritual celebration of our being sent forth from the eucharistic liturgy into the world in service of God's reign.

The council continues this missionary thrust in *Dei Verbum*. In that constitution we are told that God's Word is spoken into human history that "all may believe." The kerygmatic orientation of the council's theology of revelation led it to emphasize the power of God's Word to speak to all peoples. *Lumen Gentium* furthers this missionary perspective, describing the church as a sacrament that effects not only communion with God but also the unity of "the whole human race" (LG 1). The church is a universal sacrament of salvation (LG 48; AG 1, 5) and as such is defined by its orientation toward the world. If Christians are to be faithful to the church's mission, they must resist the temptation to stand on the sidelines of the worldly arena. The church exists entirely in order to put itself at the service of the coming reign of God. It is this missiological orientation that justifies the great missiological axiom: "the church does not have a mission, the mission has a church."[19]

We have already considered elements of this missionary imperative in the council's commitment to dialogical engagement. The council repudiated any attempt to define the church over against the world as if it were some autonomous entity, a "perfect society" (*societas perfecta*) unaffected by the issues and concerns of humankind. The church is to be a "leaven" in the world (GS 40), called to work for the world's transformation *from within*. Consequently, "one of the most important things Christians need to know about the church is that the *church* is not of ultimate importance."[20] If they are to be leaven, Christians must be willing to "get their hands dirty," to work side by side with other men and women of goodwill for the improvement of the human condition and the work for justice. Christians will do so with a particular set of convictions and motivations, of course, for they will see their work as cooperation with the grace of God and in service of the in-breaking of God's reign.

[19] Ibid., 270.

[20] Stephan B. Bevans and Roger P. Schroeder, *Constants in Context: A Theology of Mission for Today* (Maryknoll, NY: Orbis Books, 2004), 7.

VII. The Pilgrim Church

The final conciliar pillar represented, yet again, a response to the excesses of the hierocratic form of the church. The paradox of the former ecclesial form was that even as it encouraged and celebrated the call to humility and holiness through personal piety, it also manifested a harsh ecclesial triumphalism. By triumphalism I mean a pervasive assumption that the Roman Catholic Church and it alone possessed all truth and functioned as the exclusive repository of divine grace.

We see in the hierocratic Catholicism of the nineteenth and twentieth centuries a troubling ecclesial arrogance. During that period, the Catholic Church so emphasized its status as the Mystical Body of Christ on earth, instituted by Christ himself and protected from error by the Holy Spirit, that it struggled to acknowledge any divine truth, any goodness, any graced activity outside of its boundaries. Meaningful church reform was practically inconceivable.

Catholic teaching recognized, of course, that the church was comprised of both saints and sinners, and that each individual Christian was a pilgrim on a journey toward salvation. The council, however, went beyond traditional Catholic preoccupation with the "four last things" (death, heaven, hell, and final judgment) to explore the eschatological character of the church itself. The bishops taught that the church was not merely comprised of individual pilgrims on the journey toward their salvation but was itself a "pilgrim people." The image first appears in *Sacrosanctum Concilium*:

> For what marks out the church is that it is at once human and divine, visible and endowed with invisible realities, vigorously active and yet making space in its life for contemplation, present in the world and yet in pilgrimage [*peregrinam*] beyond. (SC 2)[21]

Lumen Gentium picks up this theme. While avoiding the direct attribution of sinfulness to the church, the council describes the church

[21] Translation of this excerpt from *Sacrosanctum Concilium* is from Norman P. Tanner, ed., *Decrees of the Ecumenical Councils* (Washington, DC: Georgetown University Press, 1990), 2:820. Curiously, Flannery translates *peregrinam* as "migrant" rather than "pilgrim."

as "clasping sinners to its bosom." The church requires purification and must pursue the path of "penance and renewal" (LG 8).[22]

> The church "proceeds on its pilgrim way amidst the persecutions of the world and the consolations of God," proclaiming the cross and death of the Lord until he comes. But it draws strength from the power of the risen Lord, to overcome with patience and charity its afflictions and difficulties, from within and without; and reveals his mystery faithfully in the world—albeit amid shadows—until in the end it will be made manifest in the fullness of the light. (LG 8)[23]

The theme of pilgrimage finds further exposition in chapter 7 of *Lumen Gentium*, as is evident in the very chapter title, "The Eschatological Nature of the Pilgrim Church and Its Union with the Heavenly Church." By conceiving of the church not just as a collection of individual pilgrims but as itself pilgrim, the council adopted a tone of deep eschatological humility. Thus the council could write:

> The Church, to which we are all called in Christ Jesus, and in which by the grace of God we attain holiness, will receive its perfection only in the glory of heaven, when the time for the renewal of all things will have come. (LG 48)

The church lives as a people *on the way* who have the promise of God's presence and guidance but who still await the consummation of God's plan. As a pilgrim community living in history, the church must always be willing to assess its faithfulness to the Gospel. In *Dignitatis Humanae* (The Declaration on Religious Freedom), the council admits the church's own role in ignoring the proper demands of religious freedom:

> Although, in the life of the people of God in its pilgrimage, through the vicissitudes of human history, there have at times appeared patterns of behavior which were not in keeping with the spirit of the Gospel and were even opposed to it. (DH 12)

---

[22] As Peter De Mey has noted, commentators disagree on whether LG 8 justifies attributing sinfulness to the church *qua* church. Peter De Mey, "Church Renewal and Reform in the Documents of Vatican II: History, Theology, Terminology," *The Jurist* 71 (2011): 369–400, at 372n6.

[23] The translation of this excerpt from *Lumen Gentium* is from Tanner.

We will pursue the further significance of the "pilgrim" metaphor in chapter 4.

Conclusion

These seven pillars mark out distinct contributions toward a new ecclesial form. Yet the project was left unfinished. By the fourth session the council bishops had become wearied by their time away from their home dioceses. Protracted debates with no immediate resolution led some bishops to discouragement. The compromises necessary to get the sixteen documents approved also hampered efforts to achieve a more comprehensive consistency in the council's theological vision.

There was, however, a more substantive obstacle to the completion of their project, namely, the imposing shadow that was still being cast by the hierocratic form of the church. The ruins of the old basilica, to follow Pottmeyer's metaphor, exerted a tremendous influence over the conduct of the council and, indeed, those ruins are still very much with us. We see their continued influence in a number of ecclesiastical policies and documents that emerged in the postconciliar period. Particularly during the pontificates of John Paul II and Benedict XVI, we encountered church leaders employing a more confrontational rhetoric with regular denunciations of a "dictatorship of relativism" and the secularism of the modern world. This tone is reminiscent of the siege mentality that dominated church leadership throughout the nineteenth and first half of the twentieth centuries. Second, during those two pontificates there is evidence of a preconciliar triumphalism in Vatican pronouncements like *Dominus Iesus*[24] and the 2007 Vatican statement, "Responses to Some Questions Regarding Certain Aspects of the Doctrine on the Church,"[25] statements that offered a more cautious assessment of the extent to which other Christian

[24] This document can be accessed at the Vatican website: http://www.vatican.va/roman_curia/congregations/cfaith/documents/rc_con_cfaith_doc_20000806_dominus-iesus_en.html.

[25] This document can be accessed at the Vatican website: http://www.vatican.va/roman_curia/congregations/cfaith/documents/rc_con_cfaith_doc_20070629_responsa-quaestiones_en.html.

traditions participate in the Church of Christ. Third, there were troubling signs of a neoclericalism reflected in a host of ecclesiastical documents, including the 1997 Interdicasterial document "Certain Questions Regarding Collaboration of the Non-Ordained Faithful in the Sacred Ministry of Priests,"[26] *Redemptionis Sacramentum,*[27] the revised General Instruction of the Roman Missal,[28] and even the new English translation of the Roman Missal. All of these documents, in various ways, reinforced the ontological divide between the clergy and the laity. We saw this neoclericalism at a pastoral level with the disturbing return of birettas, cassocks, and a sense of ecclesiastical entitlement in many seminarians and young priests. We have witnessed remnants of papal monarchialism in the emasculation of episcopal conferences in Pope John Paul II's apostolic letter *Apostolos Suos,*[29] in the ecclesiastical marginalization of the synod of bishops that, prior to the pontificate of Francis, had been maintained in an ecclesiastical form far less substantial than what the bishops had hoped for at the council. Finally, we find evidence of the perduring influence of the hierocratic form in the current practice in which bishops are chosen by papal appointment. This practice is a relative novelty in the history of the church and encourages a view of bishops as delegates of the pope that is, in fact, at odds with Catholic doctrine.[30]

Granting the obstacles presented by the continued influence of the hierocratic form, we must still push forward in our efforts to

[26] This document can be accessed at the Vatican website: http://www.vatican.va/roman_curia/pontifical_councils/laity/documents/rc_con_interdic_doc_15081997_en.html.

[27] This document can be accessed at the Vatican website: http://www.vatican.va/roman_curia/congregations/ccdds/documents/rc_con_ccdds_doc_20040423_redemptionis-sacramentum_en.html.

[28] This document can be accessed at the Vatican website: http://www.vatican.va/roman_curia/congregations/ccdds/documents/rc_con_ccdds_doc_20030317_ordinamento-messale_en.html.

[29] This document can be accessed at the Vatican website: http://www.vatican.va/holy_father/john_paul_ii/motu_proprio/documents/hf_jp-ii_motu-proprio_22071998_apostolos-suos_en.html.

[30] The literature on this topic is voluminous. For a recent study see, Joseph F. O'Callaghan, *Electing Our Bishops: How the Catholic Church Should Choose Its Leaders* (New York: Sheed and Ward, 2007).

further the unfinished project of the council. As I suggested in the introduction, this project will require more than a mere recitation of conciliar teaching. More coherent, integrated readings of the council are required. We must pursue synthetic accounts that strive to "connect the dots," demonstrating ways in which various conciliar teachings mutually support one another and combine to underwrite a more comprehensive program of ecclesial reform. The goal is not the construction of one master ecclesiology. The teaching of the council admits of multiple entry points, each of which, however, must draw together elements of conciliar teaching into more coherent ecclesial accounts capable of generating an effective pastoral program. The next two chapters will offer two tentative proposals in service of that goal.

4

Vatican II and the Humility
of the Church

Our first effort at "connecting the dots" of conciliar teaching will take as its starting point the final pillar treated in the last chapter, that is, the council's teaching on the humility of the church. Christian ethics has for some time made the recovery of virtue central to contemporary moral reflection. Recently, Gerard Mannion has suggested that contemporary ecclesiology follow suit, calling for a kind of "virtue ecclesiology." Such an ecclesiology would hold together what the church is and what the church does.[1] This ecclesiological perspective would be more attuned to the shape and demands of postmodernity, one that is more elastic and open to pluralism. In his 2011 plenary address to the Catholic Theological Society of America, Paul Lakeland adopted a similar tack, presenting helpful reflections on the ecclesial virtue of humility.[2] In this chapter, I would like to

[1] Gerard Mannion, *Ecclesiology and Postmodernity: Questions for the Church in Our Time* (Collegeville, MN: Liturgical Press, 2007), 195–225.

[2] Paul Lakeland, "'I Want to Be in That Number': Desire, Inclusivity and the Church," *CTSA Proceedings* 66 (2011): 16–28. Lakeland further explored Mannion's ecclesial virtue of humility in "Reflections on the Grace of Self-Doubt," in *Ecclesiology and Exclusion: Boundaries of Being and Belonging in Postmodern Times*, ed. Dennis M. Doyle, Timothy J. Furry, and Pascal D. Bazzell (Maryknoll, NY: Orbis Books, 2012), 13–17. In that same volume, see Mannion's response to Lakeland and others, "Ecclesiology and the Humility of God: Embracing the Risk of Loving the World," 24–41.

continue this line of ecclesiological inquiry, proposing that the documents of Vatican II offer a solid basis for promoting humility as an ecclesial virtue. This requires, however, some preliminary reflections on the virtue of humility itself.

I. The Virtue of Humility

In the tradition of St. Thomas Aquinas, we can define a virtue as a *stable disposition that inclines a person to act in one way or another*. Virtues are the result of positive habits that are established gradually over the course of one's life. Virtue ethics has become increasingly influential because it shifts our ethical attention from an analysis of an individual moral act to the gradual formation of moral character through certain forms of virtuous action. Within the field of virtue ethics, Lisa Fullam has made a particular case for the recovery of the virtue of humility.

Fullam argues that the virtue of humility has suffered neglect because it has been mistakenly associated with self-abasement.[3] This emphasis was particularly strong in the Augustinian tradition, where self-abasement was linked to one's sinfulness and appeared to know no limits. This was not the approach of St. Thomas Aquinas, however. For Thomas, Fullam contends, "the practice of self-abasement is not the essence of humility, just as the virtue of sobriety cannot simply be equated with abstinence from alcohol."[4] Thomas reorients his account of humility toward a pursuit of the truth of one's situation before God and the world. It serves as a salutary corrective to the innate human tendency toward "self-celebration." Following the Aristotelian pattern of seeing a virtue as the pursuit of the mean between excess and deficit, Thomas links humility not to self-deprecation but to the pursuit of honest self-knowledge.

That authentic self-knowledge is the true *telos* of humility is evident in the distinctive way that Thomas binds the virtue of humility

---

[3] Lisa Fullam, *The Virtue of Humility: A Thomistic Apologetic* (Lewiston, NY: Edwin Mellen Press, 2009), 3–4.

[4] Ibid., 4.

to the virtue of magnanimity.[5] The latter virtue is oriented toward a celebration of honor and achievement as it relates to the gifts one possesses from God. "Magnanimity makes a man deem himself worthy of great things in consideration of the gifts he holds from God."[6] Consequently, both magnanimity and humility are concerned with honest self-understanding: magnanimity honestly acknowledges one's gifts and urges one to make the greatest possible use of them, and humility honestly acknowledges one's deficiencies.[7] For Thomas, humility and magnanimity function as a kind of twofold virtue that urges one to honest self-assessment of both one's gifts and deficiencies.

Humility is an intrinsically other-centered virtue. Honest self-assessment can occur only within the framework of one's relationship with others and particularly with God.[8] Humility leads to a profound reverence for the greatness of God. It is this reverence that inevitably brings one's own failings and inadequacies into sharper focus. Humility, far from self-hatred, is simply an acknowledgment before God that I am not yet what God has called me to be. At the same time, humility is also exercised in view of the goodness of all God's creatures and the gifts that they possess. As Fullam puts it, "Humility invites us not to rest in our own gifts but to look outside ourselves and to see what else God has been up to."[9] Humility does not require that we deny our own giftedness but that we focus our attention on the giftedness of others.

James Keenan, a leading figure in the development of contemporary virtue ethics, makes his own contribution to our consideration of humility. For Keenan, the heart of the virtue lies in overcoming the vice of presumption. In this vein, Keenan will link humility with the proper exercise of power.

---

[5] Thomas relates humility to magnanimity in *Summa Theologiae* II-II, q. 161, a 1, ad. 3. He treats magnanimity directly in *Summa Theologiae* II-II, q. 129.

[6] *Summa Theologiae* II-II, q. 129, a. 3, ad 4.

[7] For a careful analysis of how Thomas correlates these two virtues see Fullam, *The Virtue of Humility*, 59–82.

[8] *Summa Theologiae* II-II, q. 161, a 1.

[9] Fullam, *The Virtue of Humility*, 132.

Humility is not self-deprecation, but rather the virtue for knowing the place of one's power in God's world. This is the humility of Jesus before Pilate, of Mary in the Magnificat, of Paul narrating his call, and of the incredible Mary Magdalene holding on to the risen Christ in the garden. In each instance they recognize their power in God's world and they do so as an act of indebtedness to the God who gave them this power. Humility is the virtue, therefore, that trains us in the exercise of that power. The more we practice humility, the more we understand the power that we, as leaders, are called to exercise.[10]

This link between humility and the exercise of power will provide a further avenue for our reflections on humility as an ecclesial virtue.

We have considered three characteristics of the virtue of humility: (1) humility and magnanimity as a kind of twofold virtue oriented toward honest self-assessment; (2) humility as an intrinsically relational and other-centered virtue, eager to celebrate the greatness of God and the gifts of others; (3) humility as concerned with the proper exercise of power. Now we must consider the possibility of an ecclesial form of the virtue of humility in council teaching.

II. Vatican II and the Humility of the Church

John O'Malley argues that one of the most distinctive features of Vatican II was its employment of a consistent rhetorical style he refers to as *panegyric,* "the painting of an idealized portrait in order to excite admiration and appropriation."[11] Recourse to this rhetorical genre, he contends, marked a departure from earlier conciliar preferences for a more juridical style of discourse, one more inclined to render legal pronouncements and canonical penalties. The council, by contrast, articulated an idealized account of the church intended to inspire believers and move the church to realize the council's vision in the practical order. In this chapter, I will argue that the council offered an account of the church's self-understanding and fundamental

[10] James F. Keenan, *Moral Wisdom: Lessons and Texts from the Catholic Tradition* (Lanham, MD: Sheed and Ward, 2010), 162–63.
[11] John W. O'Malley, *What Happened at Vatican II* (Cambridge, MA: Harvard University Press, 2008), 47.

orientation toward the world that amounts to an ecclesial form of humility and that it did so in a fashion entirely in keeping with the spirit of a panegyric.

In this chapter, our focus is on humility as an *ecclesial* virtue, but of course that presupposes that the church is itself a school of humility for its members. We can identify numerous passages in which the council called believers themselves to exercise humility. In *Apostolicam Actuositatem* (The Decree on the Apostolate of the Laity) the council exhorted the laity to imitate the humility of Christ who was not desirous of "empty glory" (AA 4). It is Christ who reveals to us the true character of Christian humility "by emptying himself" and becoming poor so that we might become rich (LG 42). By serving Christ in others, followers of Jesus may "through humility and patience bring their sisters and brothers to that King to serve whom is to reign" (LG 36). Christian missionaries are reminded that they must share the Good News of Christ with an appropriately humble spirit (AG 24). Priests, bishops, and professed religious are exhorted to give example by their humility to those to whom they serve (PO 15; CD 15; PC 5). Those who are engaged in ecumenical work are particularly admonished to exercise Christian humility in their relations with other Christians (UR 7, 11). Those undertaking advanced theological study are instructed to do so in a fashion "tempered by humility and courage in whatever branch of study they have specialized" (GS 62).

These few passages amply confirm the council's exhortation to humility addressed to individual believers. The council, however, also recognizes that it is the church itself that is called to humility (LG 8). The church must "bear in her own body the humility and the dying of Jesus" (UR 4). It is to this ecclesial exercise of humility that we must now turn our attention.

Humility and Ecclesial Self-Assessment

As we saw above, if the church is to engage in an honest self-assessment it must cultivate the virtues of both magnanimity and humility. The council exhibits this ecclesial magnanimity by affirming the gifts the church has received and which it in turn offers the world as "universal sacrament of salvation" (LG 48). In the opening chapter of *Lumen Gentium*, the council writes:

> When Jesus, having died on the cross for humanity, rose again from the dead, he appeared as Lord, Christ, and priest established forever, and he poured out on his disciples the Spirit promised by the Father. Henceforward the church, equipped with the gifts of its founder and faithfully observing his precepts of charity, humility and self-denial, receives the mission of proclaiming and establishing among all peoples the kingdom of Christ and of God, and is, on earth, the seed and the beginning of that kingdom. (LG 5)

We must note here how the council celebrated the church's gifts even as it recognized the call to humility. In several passages, the council emphasizes the fullness of the "means of sanctification and truth" that belong to the Catholic Church even as many of these elements are found "outside its visible structures" (LG 8; UR 3). It insisted that the church offers to the world the precious gift of Jesus Christ (LG 9; GS 45). At no point did the council wish to renounce this ecclesial magnanimity, which marked a substantial continuity with the hierocratic form of the church. What was most distinctive about the council's teaching, however, was not its acknowledgment of the church's many gifts but its willingness to undergo the kind of searching and critical ecclesial self-assessment that lies at the very heart of humility.

One of the most consistent features of conciliar teaching concerned the bishops' willingness to submit the church to a stringent ecclesial examination as a necessary precondition to authentic reform.[12] The commitment to serious ecclesial self-assessment makes its first appearance in Pope John XXIII's opening address. In that address, after some introductory comments on the historical role of ecumenical councils, Pope John offered his reasons for calling a new council. The church must bring herself "up to date where required." A tame statement today, but at that time such an admission was at odds with the dominant view of the church as a *societas perfecta*, a church

---

[12] For a comprehensive survey of the council's treatment of church reform, see Peter De Mey, "Church Renewal and Reform in the Documents of Vatican II: History, Theology, Terminology," *The Jurist* 71 (2011): 369–400.

hovering serenely above the turmoil of human history. It is true that "perfect," in the neoscholastic sense of the claim, meant simply that the church possessed all that was necessary for the fulfillment of its mission, but the pope chose to emphasize the church as a historical reality in need of reform and renewal. He renounced an ecclesial program built around the condemnation of error in favor of the practice of dialogue and gentle persuasion. In his concluding section, he frankly admitted the wounds of division that existed in the church and called for a new openness to ecumenism. Pope John's address introduced a new ecclesial tone at the very outset of the council. It was a tone filled with hope yet forthright in its admission that not all was well within the church. The pope sang, loudly and clearly, the first chorus in the council's plea for greater ecclesial humility.

In the very first text considered by the council bishops, the liturgy constitution, they acknowledged the need for an honest ecclesial self-assessment and placed the need for reform at the forefront of the council's deliberations:

> The sacred council has set out to impart an ever increasing vigor to the lives of the faithful; to adapt more closely to the needs of our age those institutions which are subject to change; to encourage whatever can promote the union of all who believe in Christ; to strengthen whatever serves to call all of humanity into the church's fold. Accordingly it sees particularly cogent reasons for undertaking the reform and promotion of the liturgy. (SC 1)

The liturgy constitution followed John XXIII in its forceful move beyond the post-Tridentine *societas perfecta* ecclesiology to one that was more thoroughly rooted in history.[13] The liturgy constitution was the first document to take up the image of the church as "pilgrim": "For what marks out the church is that it is at once human and divine, visible and endowed with invisible realities, vigorously active and yet making space in its life for contemplation, present in the world and yet in pilgrimage [*peregrinam*] beyond" (SC 2).[14]

---

[13] Massimo Faggioli, *True Reform: Liturgy and Ecclesiology in* Sacrosanctum Concilium (Collegeville, MN: Liturgical Press, 2012), 83.

[14] Translation from Norman P. Tanner, ed., *Decrees of the Ecumenical Councils* (Washington, DC: Georgetown University Press, 1990), 2:820.

The image reinforces a sense of the church's historical embeddedness that, in turn, opens up the possibility of authentic reform:

> The liturgy is made up of unchangeable elements divinely instituted, and of elements subject to change. These latter not only may be changed but ought to be changed with the passage of time, if they have suffered from the intrusion of anything out of harmony with the inner nature of the liturgy or have become less suitable. (SC 21)

The reality of historical change extends to the liturgical rites themselves: "The council also desires that, where necessary the rites be revised carefully in the light of sound tradition, and that they be given new vigor to meet present-day circumstances" (SC 4). Regarding the Eucharist, in particular, the bishops insisted that liturgical revisions be undertaken such that

> the intrinsic nature and purpose of its several parts, as well as the connection between them, may be more clearly shown, and that devout and active participation by the faithful may be more easily achieved. To this end, the rites are to be simplified, due care being taken to preserve their substance. Duplications made with the passage of time are to be omitted, as are less useful additions. Other parts which were lost through the vicissitudes of history are to be restored according to the ancient tradition of the holy Fathers, as may seem appropriate or necessary. (SC 50)

The ecclesial self-assessment that promotes ecclesial humility is further explored in the Dogmatic Constitution on the Church. *Lumen Gentium* describes the church as "clasping sinners to its bosom." The painful presence of sin in the church demands purification and the ecclesial pursuit of the path of "penance and renewal" (LG 8). For the council, this is the inevitable path of human pilgrimage:

> The church "proceeds on its pilgrim way amidst the persecutions of the world and the consolations of God," proclaiming the cross and death of the Lord until he comes. But it draws strength from the power of the risen Lord, to overcome with patience and charity its afflictions and difficulties, from within and without; and reveals his mystery faithfully in the world—albeit amid shadows—until in the end it will be made manifest in the fullness of the light. (LG 8)[15]

---

[15] The translation is from Tanner, *Decrees of the Ecumenical Councils.*

This rigorous examination of church conduct, past and present, is also displayed in the Decree on Ecumenism, *Unitatis Redintegratio*: "In this one and only church of God from its very beginnings there arose certain rifts, which the Apostle strongly censures as damnable. But in subsequent centuries much more serious dissensions appeared and large communities became separated from full communion with the Catholic Church—for which, often enough, people on both sides were to blame" (UR 3).

An honest consideration of the church's failings is, according to the council, a necessary precondition for any genuine ecumenical endeavor. The bishops wrote that the primary ecumenical duty of Catholics was "to make a careful and honest appraisal of whatever needs to be renewed and done in the catholic household itself, in order that its life may bear witness more clearly and more faithfully to the teachings and institutions which have been handed down from Christ through the apostles" (UR 4).

The ecumenical decree then specifies what getting the "Catholic household" in order may require:

> Every renewal of the church essentially consists in an increase of fidelity to her own calling. Undoubtedly this explains the dynamism of the movement toward unity. Christ summons the church, as she goes her pilgrim way, to that continual reformation of which she always has need, insofar as she is a human institution. Consequently, if, in various times and circumstances, there have been deficiencies in moral conduct or in church discipline, or even in the way that church teaching has been formulated—to be carefully distinguished from the deposit of faith itself—these should be set right at the opportune moment and in the proper way. (UR 6)

The council largely abandoned a preconciliar conception of a static and immutable church residing safely on some ethereal plane in favor of a more historically grounded account of the church. The bishops thus conjoined the preconciliar emphasis on the magnanimity of the church with a bold new commitment to ecclesial humility and the need for a rigorously critical self-assessment. Only a balanced appreciation of the tethered ecclesial virtues of humility and magnanimity can steer our church between two corresponding excesses: the neotriumphalism of certain Catholic apologetics and the indiscriminate church bashing of both the secular media and the Catholic commentariat's extreme left.

Humility and Other-Centeredness

The second characteristic of the virtue of humility concerns its relational other-centeredness; humility habituates us to focus not on our own accomplishments but on the other and, preeminently, on the divine Other. Transposed into an ecclesial key, a truly humble church would eschew any form of ecclesial triumphalism and, in the place of ecclesial self-congratulation, would give prominence to the church's utter dependence for its life and mission on the triune life of God. Vatican II moved decisively in this direction, repudiating ecclesial triumphalism time and again and effectively grounding the life and mission of the church in the trinitarian missions of Word and Spirit. This transposition is most evident in *Dei Verbum* (The Dogmatic Constitution on Divine Revelation). Consider the opening passage of the constitution:

> Hearing the word of God reverently and proclaiming it confidently, this holy synod makes its own the words of St. John: "We proclaim to you the eternal life which was with the Father and was made manifest to us—that which we have seen and heard we proclaim also to you, so that you may have fellowship with us; and our fellowship is with the Father and with his Son Jesus Christ." (DV 1)

Before the church can preach or teach with any integrity it must first listen. It is in view of this ecclesial receptivity that the council will acknowledge that all the Christian faithful are given that supernatural instinct for the faith, the *sensus fidei*, to allow them to receive God's Word, penetrate its meaning, and apply it more fully in their lives (LG 12). Dependence on the revelatory Word led the council to insist that although the task of giving an authoritative interpretation of the Word of God is entrusted to the magisterium, "this magisterium is not superior to the word of God, but is rather its servant" (DV 10).

Dei Verbum offers a theology of revelation grounded in the divine invitation to friendship. The church is called into communion with God in Christ:

> By this revelation, then, the invisible God, from the fullness of his love, addresses men and women as his friends and lives among them, in order to invite and receive them into his own company. . . . The most intimate truth thus revealed about God and human salvation shines forth for us in Christ, who is himself both the mediator and the sum total of revelation. (DV 2)

The Christo-centrism evident in this passage plays an important role in the council's evocation of a humbler church more aware of its radical dependence on God's saving work. Too often overlooked are the many conciliar texts that ground the life and mission of the church in Christ.[16] Some forget that the Latin title of the Dogmatic Constitution on the Church, *Lumen Gentium*, "light of the nations," refers not to the church but to Christ. That constitution opens with these lines: "Christ is the light of the nations and consequently this holy synod, gathered together in the holy Spirit, ardently desires to bring to all humanity that light of Christ which is resplendent on the face of the church, by proclaiming his Gospel to every creature" (LG 1). The church is to be focused not on itself but on Christ, the subject of the church's proclamation.

Even as the council insisted on the centrality of Christ, it avoided as well a reductive ecclesial christomonism by also recalling the mission of the Holy Spirit. *Dei Verbum* develops the fully trinitarian shape of divine revelation, asserting that the church's response and reception of the divine Word is dependent on the action of the Spirit, "who moves the heart and converts it to God, and opens the eyes of the mind and makes it easy for all to accept and believe the truth" (DV 5). Ormond Rush has developed a rich theology of ecclesial reception built on the conciliar teaching that it is the function of the Holy Spirit to bring "to realization God's revelatory and salvific purposes."[17] The Holy Spirit constitutes the church as a community of reception, wherein its humility derives from its gratitude for what it has received from the divine Other revealed in Christ by the power of the Spirit.

---

[16] One sees the christological grounding of the church in such texts as SC 2, 7; GS 22, 45; NA 4; PO 5; OT 16.

[17] Ormond Rush, *The Eyes of Faith: The Sense of the Faithful and the Church's Reception of Revelation* (Washington, DC: The Catholic University of America Press, 2009), 26.

This reception must not be imagined as if it were a one-time event. It is not the case that the church simply received Christ at some definitive point in the past such that what was once received is now in its firm possession. Rather, since what is received in the event of revelation is not, in the first instance, propositional information but the offer of divine communion, the church's posture of receptivity and dependence is characteristic of its entire historical existence. The council affirms this in the second chapter of *Dei Verbum*, "The Transmission of Divine Revelation." There, the bishops present Scripture and tradition as a kind of mirror "in which the church, during its pilgrim journey here on earth, contemplates God, from whom it receives everything, until such time as it is brought to see him face to face as he really is" (DV 7).

Here we encounter a form of "doctrinal humility," far removed from that of the hierocratic church form. Catherine Cornille notes that, in the past, when humility was related to doctrine, "it has more often been regarded as an attitude to be adopted *toward* rather than *about* the truth of Christian doctrines."[18] Individual Christians were reminded of the limits of human reason and exhorted to a humble posture of docile obedience in the face of the authority of doctrine. Yet, the council invites us to an altogether different form of doctrinal humility. *Dei Verbum* 8 presents a dynamic account of tradition's development and then offers the remarkable admission that the church lives in history, moving "toward the plenitude of divine truth." This brief clause presents revealed truth as both historically conditioned and subject to eschatological fulfillment. The church does not so much possess revelation as it is possessed by it; the church is called to live into divine truth.

This doctrinal humility is evident in the council's presentation of the hierarchy of truths in *Unitatis Redintegratio* 11: "When comparing doctrines with one another, they should remember that in Catholic doctrine there exists an order or 'hierarchy' of truths, since they vary in their relation to the foundation of the Christian faith."

The "foundation of the Christian faith" refers to divine revelation itself. The doctrinal humility that the council encouraged leads us away from any arrogant claim that church doctrine provides a com-

[18] Catherine Cornille, *The Im-possibility of Interreligious Dialogue* (New York: Crossroad, 2008), 27–28.

prehensive grasp of divine revelation in favor of a stance of receptivity toward the revealing God. Doctrine does symbolically mediate divine revelation; it does not exhaust it.

The council's deep humility is evident as well in its treatment of modern atheism. Rather than simply denouncing it, the council acknowledged that, in some sense,

> Everybody remains a question to themselves, one that is dimly perceived and left unanswered. For there are times, especially in the major events of life, when nobody can altogether escape from such self-questioning. God alone, who calls people to deeper thought and to more humble probing, can fully and with complete certainty supply an answer to this questioning. (GS 21)

The atheist's own questions may be a response to God's call to "deeper thought and to more humble probing." This call for doctrinal humility brings together two pillars of conciliar teaching, the church's pilgrim status and its theology of revelation as an openness to a personal encounter with God as mystery.

The other-centered character of humility is not limited to the church's receptive stance toward God but extends as well to an appreciation of the created "other." Ecclesial humility is the condition for the possibility of yet another pillar of conciliar teaching, the council's commitment to dialogical engagement. Pope Paul VI's first encyclical, *Ecclesiam Suam*, was promulgated a month or so prior to the third session of the council. The encyclical was dedicated almost entirely to a dialogical vision of the church; it exerted a pronounced influence on conciliar deliberations. In *Gaudium et Spes* we find an exhortation to intraecclesial dialogue:

> Such a mission requires us first of all to create in the church itself mutual esteem, reverence and harmony, and to acknowledge all legitimate diversity; in this way all who constitute the one people of God will be able to engage in ever more fruitful dialogue, whether they are pastors or other members of the faithful. For the ties which unite the faithful together are stronger than those which separate them: let there be unity in what is necessary, freedom in what is doubtful, and charity in everything. (GS 92)

Intraecclesial dialogue, that is, dialogue within the Catholic Church, presumes a shared commitment to the apostolic faith, the "unity in what is necessary." Yet at the same time, it is both this unity in essentials and the "charity in everything" that frees the church to be open to dialogue on "doubtful matters."

How different would Catholic life be today if we were to embrace this freedom to enter into conversation regarding doubtful matters? Modern Catholicism has long been paralyzed by the possibility of doubt, doctrinal questioning, and lively, substantive disagreement. Dissenting theological positions are condemned because of the danger of "confusing the faithful." The patronizing assumption here is that honest disagreement and doubt will lead to confusion, the enemy of authentic Christian faith. But might not confusion be the appropriate response to church positions that are no longer compelling and fairly beg honest questions? Might not doubt shed light on church arguments that are no longer compelling and official positions that might benefit from greater scrutiny? A humble church would recognize the positive potential of doubt, confusion, and disagreement when they emerge in conversations dedicated to the pursuit of truth wherever it is found.

This spirit of humble dialogue was carried over into the Catholic encounters with other Christians in ecumenical relationships. This dialogue requires, on the part of Catholics, that they "become familiar with the outlook of the separated churches and communities" (UR 9). The dialogical imperative was extended as well to those who belong to non-Christian religions. The council asserted that the origins of the religious traditions of the world often lie in the effort to seek answers to the great questions that have long preoccupied the human spirit (NA 1). In *Nostra Aetate* (The Declaration on the Relation of the Church to Non-Christian Religions), the council affirmed that, in these great religions, one can find "a ray of that truth which enlightens all men and women" and it exhorted Catholics to prudent and charitable "discussion and collaboration with members of other religions" (NA 2). Finally, we must acknowledge the dialogical spirit manifested in the council's attitude toward the world itself. In the pastoral constitution we find a key text that captures the council's deep ecclesial humility:

> The church is guardian of the deposit of God's word and draws religious and moral principles from it, but it does not always have a ready answer to every question. Still, it is eager to associate the light of revelation

with the experience of humanity in trying to clarify the course upon which it has recently entered. (GS 33)

The church can claim genuine insight, drawn from revelation, without pretending it is a divinely sanctioned "answer box" for all the world's problems. This passage establishes the fundamental rationale for dialogue with the world: the church has both something to offer and something to learn from the world.

> Just as it is in the world's interest to acknowledge the church as a social reality and a driving force in history, so too the church is not unaware how much it has profited from the history and development of humankind. It profits from the experience of past ages, from the progress of the sciences, and from the riches hidden in various cultures, through which greater light is thrown on human nature and new avenues to truth are opened up. (GS 44)

This openness and receptivity to the world manifests that radical other-centeredness that is essential to the virtue of ecclesial humility.

Humility and the Exercise of Power

Finally, we turn to the third characteristic of the virtue of humility. As Keenan reminded us, humility is the virtue that trains us in the exercise of power. A church that lives out of the virtue of humility will be a church that exercises power and authority in imitation of Christ who saw power and authority as service.

All ecclesial power is in some sense a participation in the presence and activity of the Spirit in the life of the church. According to the council, it is the Holy Spirit who "guides the church in the way of all truth and, uniting it in fellowship and ministry, bestows upon it different hierarchic and charismatic gifts, and in this way directs it and adorns it with his fruits. By the power of the Gospel he rejuvenates the church, constantly renewing it and leading it to perfect union with its spouse" (LG 4).

By baptism, all the *Christifideles* are empowered by the Spirit for Christian life and ministry. Within the life of the church, "power" can be thought of as the Spirit enabling Christians to fulfill their baptismal call and engage in effective action in service of the church's life and mission.

The council did not offer any developed theological reflections on the relationship between baptismal empowerment and the particular empowerment that occurs by way of ministerial ordination. Yet, it did insist that the exercise of ministerial power is always in service of the mission of the people of God. Power is never exercised for its own sake. The council avoided the typical neoscholastic debates regarding the proper scope and limits for the exercise of jurisdictional power or concerning the relationship between the power of orders and the power of jurisdiction. Rather, it directed its attention toward the exercise of ministerial power configured for Christian service. Consider this key text in *Lumen Gentium*, introducing the chapter on the hierarchical character of the church:

> In order to ensure that the people of God would have pastors and would enjoy continual growth, Christ the Lord set up in his church a variety of offices whose aim is the good of the whole body. Ministers, invested with sacred power, *are at the service of their brothers and sisters*, so that all who belong to the people of God and therefore enjoy true Christian dignity may attain to salvation through their free, combined and well-ordered efforts in pursuit of a common goal. (LG 18, emphasis mine)

A few paragraphs down, the council returns to this sense of ministerial power as service: "The bishops, therefore, have undertaken along with their fellow-workers, the priests and deacons, *the service of the community*" (LG 20, emphasis mine).[19] In *Presbyterorum Ordinis*, the power conferred on priests by ordination, the council teaches, is "a power whose purpose is to build up the church. And in building up the church priests ought to treat everybody with the greatest kindness after the example of our Lord" (PO 6). The council insists that "priests, in common with all who have been reborn in the font of Baptism, are brothers and sisters as members of the same body of Christ which all are commanded to build" (PO 9). The ministerial leadership of the priest requires that they "unite their efforts with those of the lay faithful."

> Priests are to be sincere in their appreciation and promotion of lay people's dignity and of the special role the laity have to play in the

---

[19] Translation from Tanner, *Decrees of the Ecumenical Councils*.

church's mission. . . . They should be willing to listen to lay people, give brotherly consideration to their wishes, and recognize their experience and competence in the different fields of human activity. . . . While testing the spirits to discover if they be of God, they must discover with faith, recognize with joy, and foster diligently the many and varied charismatic gifts of the laity, whether these be of a humble or more exalted kind. Among the other gifts of God which are found abundantly among the faithful. . . . Priests should confidently entrust to the laity duties in the service of the church, giving them freedom and opportunity for activity and even inviting them, when opportunity offers, to undertake projects on their own initiative. (PO 9; see also AA 3)

Almost completely absent from the council documents is any notion of ministerial power presented as either a coercive/punitive power over others or as a matter of simply "ruling" over others. Rather, the council consistently opted for the language of service and collaboration, and in the place of "ruling imagery" we find instead the dominance of the pastoral image of shepherding and its associative responsibilities to learn and care for one's flock (CD 11, 16).

In this chapter I have proposed a reading of the council's teaching that draws together several conciliar "pillars" (the church as pilgrim, the council's theology of revelation as an invitation to doctrinal humility, and the call for dialogical engagement) in order to propose a theological account of a church deeply shaped by ecclesial humility. Fifty years later, the council's vision of a magnanimous yet humble church stands before us today as both a challenge and, sadly, a reproach. The pursuit of this kind of more synthetic reading of the council will lead, one hopes, to a more coherent program for church reform and renewal. I will consider some features of such a program in more detail in the final chapter. In the next chapter, however, I will offer a complementary account of council teaching that emphasizes, as a principle for synthesizing the council's teaching, a noncompetitive account of the church.

5

A Noncompetitive Theology
of the Church

A consistent claim of this volume is that, five decades removed from Vatican II, there is work still to be done to produce more synthetic interpretations of council teaching that yield a coherent vision of the church and a commensurate program for church reform. Chapter 4 pursued this project from the perspective of the tethered ecclesial virtues of magnanimity and humility. In this chapter, we turn to the council's recovery of pneumatology, a theology of the Holy Spirit, as a complementary organizing principle. The council's recovery of the role of the Holy Spirit in the life of the church brings into sharper relief an integrative ecclesiological theme that lies just below the surface of council teaching, namely, a noncompetitive theology of the church. The term "noncompetitive" is not found in the council documents, yet I will argue that the term aptly describes the way the council overcame the hierocratic church's tendency to pit key ecclesial elements in competitive, oppositional relationships.

I. The Modern Emergence of Competitive Theologies

I have borrowed the language of a noncompetitive theology from the work of the Protestant theologian Kathryn Tanner, who has developed a theology of grace that provides the basis for what she has called a noncompetitive theology of Christian life.[1] For Tanner, such

[1] Kathryn Tanner, *The Politics of God: Christian Theologies and Social Justice* (Minneapolis, MN: Fortress Press, 1992); Kathryn Tanner, *Economy of Grace* (Minneapolis, MN: Fortress Press, 2005).

a theology is grounded in God's unmerited gift of God's self to us. This grace never becomes our private possession but is received and shared in gratitude. Since grace is not a commodity to be measured, it cannot be the basis for a competitive relationship among creatures. Our lives are themselves sites of God's self-giving action. Christians are to live in imitation of the divine gift-giving in which God, in giving away God's very self, does not become any less God.[2] God's giving does not create lack within God because what is given transcends quantification. So too, we, God's creatures, acknowledging our own giftedness, are to imitate God's gift-giving in our relations with one another. What we give to and for one another is also beyond quantification and therefore does not contribute any lack or debt of the kind that would require a commensurable exchange.

In several of her works, Tanner applies this principle of noncompetition to the field of social ethics but with relatively little consideration of its implications for ecclesiology. Recently, the Catholic theologian John Thiel appropriated elements of Tanner's work and proposed that Vatican II's teaching on the universal call to holiness, the baptismal priesthood, and a more optimistic theology of the salvation of nonbelievers reflected the emergence of a noncompetitive theological framework in modern Catholicism.[3] In this chapter, I will pursue the possibility that Vatican II consistently transposed oppositional ecclesial relationships into noncompetitive ecclesial relationships, largely by way of its recovery of a theology of the Holy Spirit.

II. Vatican II's Development of a Noncompetitive Theology of the Church

The church is structured around a great diversity of roles and responsibilities, yet throughout history Christians have too often succumbed to the temptation to configure these diverse roles and

[2] Kathryn Tanner, *Jesus, Humanity and the Trinity: A Brief Systematic Theology* (Minneapolis, MN: Fortress Press, 2001), 90.

[3] John Thiel, *Icons of Hope: The Last Things in Catholic Imagination* (Notre Dame, IN: University of Notre Dame Press, 2013).

responsibilities in competitive hierarchical "economies" constituted by pervasive power inequities. Vatican II's substantial, if not entirely consistent, recovery of pneumatology allowed it to move toward a transformative, noncompetitive ecclesiology.

The council's tentative reappropriation of a more pneumatological ecclesiology represented an advance beyond the mystical body ecclesiology that emerged in the nineteenth and early twentieth centuries and was affirmed by Pius XII in his encyclical *Mystici Corporis*. This preconciliar view of the church as the Mystical Body of Christ saw the role of the Holy Spirit largely as the animating soul of the ecclesial body. The difficulty with this approach, which admittedly is not entirely absent from the council documents, is that it positions the Spirit as a secondary adjunct to Christ; the Spirit is the trinitarian person who comes along later to animate what Christ has already established. A more adequate theology will recognize what Congar called the coinstituting character of both Word and Spirit in the life of the church. This theology provides the foundation for a noncompetitive account of ecclesial relationships.[4] This noncompetitive framework is evident in the council's treatment of four distinct relational pairs.

Toward a Noncompetitive Theology of the Relationship between Pope and Bishops

As we saw in chapter 1, over the course of the second millennium, the papacy grew in power and acquired imperial and monarchial trappings that often obscured its ancient role as a servant and guarantor of the church's faith and communion. As a consequence of the papal paranoia occasioned by the conciliarist crisis, it became impossible to assert any real authority for regional groupings of bishops. The assertions of limited ecclesiastical autonomy for bishops gathering regionally in the seventeenth and eighteenth centuries (e.g., Gallicanism and Febronianism) were cast as new forms of conciliarism

---

[4] Congar would, in his more mature work on pneumatology, insist that it was not enough to speak of the Spirit animating a church already established in its institutional structures by Christ. The Holy Spirit worked in history as a coinstituting principle in the development of those institutional church structures. See Yves Congar, "The Two Missions: The Spirit as the Co-Instituting Principle of the Church," in *I Believe in the Holy Spirit* (New York: Seabury, 1983), 2:7.

and denounced vigorously by pope after pope as an attack on papal authority. A program of increased papal centralism gradually transformed bishops into little more than spiritual vicars of the pope. This view was strengthened considerably when, in the nineteenth century, the papacy dramatically expanded the practice of papal appointment of bishops to local churches. When only the pope appoints a bishop and only a pope can remove one, it is hard not to see a bishop as little more than a papal delegate. What emerged over the course of the second millennium was a competitive, zero-sum relationship between pope and bishops. To assert the authority of one inevitably entailed the diminishment of the authority of the other.

Vatican II's teaching on episcopal collegiality represents an important if not entirely successful move away from this competitive schema. It did so by way of a renewed theology of the local church and a greater stress on the bishop's role within the local church. The council's presentation of the local church and its relation to the universal church, however inconsistent, constituted nothing less than what Joseph Komonchak once referred to as a "Copernican revolution in ecclesiology."[5] Beginning with the eucharistic ecclesiology of *Sacrosanctum Concilium*, the council offered a theological account of the local church as something other than a "branch office" of the universal church. It is in the local church where the people of God gather for the proclamation of the Word and the breaking of the bread under the presidency of an apostolic minister and from which they are sent into the world in mission. Since it is the Eucharist that constitutes the local church, a theology of the universal church appears not as an abstract universal entity but as a spiritual communion of eucharistic communions. And it is the Holy Spirit that acts as the divine agent of that communion (see LG 13, 25, 49; UR 2; AG 19).

From this recovery of the local church came a theology of the bishop as something other than a vicar of the pope; the council taught that the bishop is the ordinary pastor of the local church (LG 27). According to *Sacrosanctum Concilium*, the local church finds its most visible expression at diocesan liturgies presided over by the bishop:

---

[5] Joseph A. Komonchak, "Ministry and the Local Church," *CTSA Proceedings* 36 (1981): 58.

> Therefore, all should hold in great esteem the liturgical life of the dio-
> cese centered around the bishop, especially in his cathedral church.
> They must be convinced that the principal manifestation of the church
> consists in the full, active participation of all God's holy people in the
> same liturgical celebrations, especially in the same Eucharist, in a single
> prayer, at one altar, at which the bishop presides, surrounded by his
> college of priests and by his ministers. (SC 41)

The bishop's ministry is best apprehended not by way of some ab-
stract analysis of the sacramental powers conferred on the bishop at
his consecration, but by way of his pastoral relationship to his flock.
This relationship is ritually enacted in the bishop's presidency at the
Eucharist. The council develops this further in the Decree on the
Pastoral Office of the Bishop:

> A diocese is a [portion] of God's people entrusted to a bishop to be
> guided by him with the [the cooperation of his priests] so that, loyal
> to its pastor and formed by him into one community in the holy Spirit
> through the Gospel and the Eucharist, it constitutes one particular
> church in which the one, holy, catholic and apostolic church of Christ
> is truly present and active. (CD 11)

A relational view of episcopal ministry is then extended to the bishop's relationship to his fellow bishops in the episcopal college:

> Individual bishops are the visible source and foundation of unity in their
> own particular churches, which are modelled on the universal church;
> it is in and from these that the one and unique catholic church exists.
> And for that reason each bishop represents his own church, whereas all
> of them together with the pope represent the whole church in a bond
> of peace, love and unity. (LG 23)

Note the significance here of the pope being placed *within* the college of bishops as both head and member. Even in its treatment of
the teaching authority of the pope and bishops, *Lumen Gentium*
25 begins first with the teaching authority of the college of bishops
before considering that of the pope. Vatican II affirmed Vatican I's
teaching on papal primacy but did so by situating that primacy within
the larger context of the entire episcopal college.

   This shift provided the decisive theological foundation for the
council's teaching on episcopal collegiality, namely, its teaching that

although the college of bishops has no authority on its own apart from communion with its head, the pope, nevertheless, the college shares with the Bishop of Rome, and never apart from him, "supreme and full power over the universal church" (LG 22). By making the doctrine of episcopal collegiality the context for a consideration of papal teaching authority, the council provided a noncompetitive framework for the pope/bishop relationship. Even when the pope exercised his authority apart from the explicit cooperation of the bishops, his actions presume an enduring communion between the pope and the college. In fact, the ecclesiological thrust of this position has led some postconciliar commentators to insist that there is but one subject of supreme authority in the church and that is the college of bishops with the Bishop of Rome as its necessary head. This position does not deny that this authority may be exercised according to different modalities: either the college as a whole or the pope as head and member of the college.

Unfortunately, the many compromises made to mollify the conservative minority, particularly the juridical rendering of collegiality articulated in the *nota praevia* attached to chapter 3 of *Lumen Gentium*, weakened the force of this development. The council minority feared that the emerging teaching on collegiality would undermine Vatican I's teaching on papal primacy. There can be no doubt that a fuller treatment of the liturgical context of episcopal ministry, hinted at in SC 41, would have placed the ministry of the bishops and their relationship with the bishop of Rome within a more adequate, trinitarian framework. This framework would have brought out the full theological implications of a noncompetitive theology of the relationship between pope and bishops. Nevertheless, what we see in the council's teaching on episcopal collegiality is a move from a competitive to a noncompetitive account of the relationship between pope and bishops.

Two postconciliar documents have offered more promise in this regard. The first is a much-overlooked 1982 ecumenical document produced by the Joint Commission for Dialogue between the Roman Catholic Church and the Orthodox Church titled "The Mystery of the Church and the Eucharist in the Light of the Mystery of the Holy Trinity."[6] There, the liturgical context for the ministry of the bishop

---

[6] Joint Commission for Dialogue between the Roman Catholic Church and the Orthodox Church, "The Mystery of the Church and the Eucharist

is given rich expression. At the eucharistic synaxis, it is the bishop who presides over the *koinonia* of the eucharistic assembly, a *koinonia* in turn grounded in the *koinonia* of the triune God. Episcopal ordination is not about the conferral of power but the insertion into a ministry of service to the *koinonia* of the church. And since this ecclesial *koinonia* is not limited to the local church, but extends to the *koinonia* among all the churches, so too the bishop's ministry of service extends to his communion with his brother bishops, including, it would follow, the Bishop of Rome.

We find further hints of a noncompetitive account of the pope-bishop relationship in Pope John Paul II's encyclical on ecumenism, *Ut Unum Sint*. The pope there describes the relationship of the pope to the bishops:

> This service of unity, rooted in the action of divine mercy, is entrusted within the College of Bishops to one among those who have received from the Spirit the task, not of exercising power over the people—as the rulers of the Gentiles and their great men do—but of leading them towards peaceful pastures.[7]

It is the Holy Spirit that establishes a noncompetitive relationship among the bishops and between bishops and the Christian faithful.

Unfortunately, in spite of this remarkable document, the pontificates of John Paul II and Benedict XVI were responsible for a dramatic retrenchment. The two principal postconciliar institutions intended to operationalize the council's teaching on collegiality were emasculated—episcopal conferences and the synod of bishops. Pope John Paul II's 1998 apostolic letter *Apostolos Suos*[8] significantly restricted the doctrinal teaching authority of episcopal conferences. The synod

---

in the Light of the Mystery of the Holy Trinity," available online at http://www.vatican.va/roman_curia/pontifical_councils/chrstuni/ch_orthodox_docs/rc_pc_chrstuni_doc_19820706_munich_en.html.

[7] John Paul II, Encyclical Letter *Ut Unum Sint*, 94, available online at http://www.vatican.va/holy_father/john_paul_ii/encyclicals/documents/hf_jp-ii_enc_25051995_ut-unum-sint_en.html.

[8] John Paul II, Apostolic Letter *Apostolos Suos*, available online at http://www.vatican.va/holy_father/john_paul_ii/motu_proprio/documents/hf_jp-ii_motu-proprio_22071998_apostolos-suos_en.html.

of bishops, as conceived in Pope Paul VI's *Apostolica Solicitudo*,[9] was a far cry from the permanent synod envisioned by many of the council fathers. After 1971, it was left to the pope to give expression to the fruit of any given synod in the promulgation of a postsynodal apostolic exhortation. Over the course of the successive pontificates of John Paul II and Benedict XVI, the postconciliar synods were carefully scripted and regulated by the Curia. As we shall see in the next chapter, Pope Francis is determined to reinvigorate the role of both episcopal conferences and synods as part of his commitment to a program of papal decentralization.

Toward a Noncompetitive Theology of the Relationship of the Magisterium and the Whole Christian Faithful

A second instance of the council's shift from a competitive to a noncompetitive theology of the church concerns the very handing on of the Christian faith. It was Pius X who, in 1906, described the church as an unequal society comprised of two ranks, the clergy and the laity. With the bishops lay the exclusive responsibility to teach the faith. Presupposed here was a centuries-old distinction between the teaching church (*ecclesia docens*) and the learning church (*ecclesia discens*). Neoscholastic theologies treated divine revelation as a *depositum fidei*, a somewhat unfortunate formulation that, while retaining a legitimate truth, risked distorting revelation by suggesting a quantitative collection of truths. Quantifiable conceptions of revelation made it easier to imagine revelation as something that could be possessed and mastered. This more propositional understanding of revelation hinted at an ecclesiastical Gnosticism in which the pope and bishops were the exclusive repositories of divine truth who then handed these truths on to the rest of us. Yet, this theology has tenuous roots in the Catholic tradition. Bishops, in fact, do not receive supernaturally infused knowledge of divine revelation at their ordination. The bishops are given a special assistance of the Holy Spirit (*charisma veritatis*) in their ministry to preserve that apostolic faith

[9] Paul VI, Apostolic Letter *Apostolica Solicitudo*, available online at: http://www.vatican.va/holy_father/paul_vi/motu_proprio/documents/hf_p-vi_motu-proprio_19650915_apostolica-sollicitudo_en.html.

given to the whole church. The neoscholastic, propositional view of revelation reflects another manifestation of a competitive theological framework in which one posits a finite set of truths that are in the exclusive possession of the magisterium. Any claim that the faithful or theologians would have their own access to those truths would compromise the distinctive claims of the magisterium. This competitive framework also explains the harsh disciplinary actions of the magisterium directed toward dissenting theologians; if the magisterium is the exclusive repository of divine truth, then it must squelch any "competing" claims to truth.

Here again the council points the way toward a noncompetitive framework by way of a trinitarian theology of revelation and a more robust theology of the Holy Spirit. This is evident in the very opening line of *Dei Verbum*: "Hearing the word of God with reverence and proclaiming it with faith, the sacred synod takes its direction from these words of St. John . . ." (DV 1). Revelation, the council teaches, begins not with a collection of doctrines but with God's Word. This Word is offered as an event of divine self-communication. In divine revelation, God "addresses us as friends" and invites us into communion. Then it asserts, "by this revelation then, the deepest truth about God and the salvation of humanity shines out for our sake in Christ, who is both the mediator and the fullness of all revelation" (DV 2). The knowledge of God that has been revealed to us in Christ is the kind of knowledge gained in personal relationship. We come to know God through our relationship with Christ and in his Spirit. Revelation comes to us in the person of Christ and, as such, it is received by the whole church, albeit in different ways. According to council teaching, the magisterium has the exclusive responsibility to safeguard the apostolic faith through its authoritative teaching but, as the council also taught:

> This teaching office is not above the word of God, but serves it, teaching only what has been handed on, listening to it devoutly, guarding it scrupulously and explaining it faithfully in accord with a divine commission and with the help of the Holy Spirit. (DV 10)

The council resisted any claim that the magisterium had an *exclusive* role to play in the transmission of the apostolic faith. According to the council, all the Christian faithful play a role in receiving God's

Word. *Lumen Gentium* 12 teaches that every Christian, by virtue of their baptism, receives a supernatural instinct for the faith through which "the people of God adheres unwaveringly to the faith given once and for all to the saints, penetrates it more deeply with right thinking, and applies it more fully in its life." This insight appears as well in *Dei Verbum*'s articulation of the ecclesial processes that allow tradition to grow and develop:

> This comes about through the contemplation and study of believers who ponder these things in their hearts. It comes from the intimate sense of spiritual realities which they experience, and through the preaching of those who have received through Episcopal succession the sure gift of truth. (DV 8)

In these various passages, we see a theology of a listening church, one in which all believers should contribute to the development of tradition. Since the same Spirit that guides the magisterium confers on all believers the *sensus fidei*, there can be no competition between the contributions of the bishops and those of ordinary Christian faithful (or theologians). Further evidence of this noncompetitive understanding of the traditioning process is fully displayed in *Gaudium et Spes* 44:

> With the help of the holy Spirit, it is the task of the whole people of God, particularly of its pastors and theologians, to listen to and distinguish the many voices of our times and to interpret them in the light of God's word, in order that the revealed truth may be more deeply penetrated, better understood, and more suitably presented.

This noncompetitive understanding of the complex processes by which the church receives God's Word will be further developed by John Paul II, who in his apostolic letter *Novo Millennio Ineunte* quotes St. Paulinus of Nola: "Let us listen to what all the faithful say, because in every one of them the Spirit of God breathes" (NM 45). Later in an address to the US bishops in September 2004, the pope went even further:

> A commitment to creating better structures of participation, consultation, and shared responsibility, should not be misunderstood as a concession to a secular democratic model of governance, but as an

intrinsic requirement of the exercise of episcopal authority and a necessary means of strengthening that authority.[10]

It is difficult to ignore the unusually strong language: consultation is an "intrinsic requirement" of the exercise of church authority. There is no competition between the magisterium and the rest of the Christian faithful; all belong to a listening church.

The 1983 Code of Canon Law, in canon 212, explicitly affirms the rights of the faithful to make known their needs and desires and to share their insight with church leaders. In keeping with this fundamental right, the code provides several consultative structures oriented toward input from the Christian faithful.[11] For example, the code encourages the creation of diocesan pastoral councils (c. 511) and the convocation of diocesan synods (cc. 460–68); in both instances lay participation is envisioned. It must also be noted, however, that these structures are only *recommended* by the code, whereas diocesan presbyteral councils are actually mandated by canon law (c. 495). There is another structure mandated by the code that, in principle, could offer an important venue for consultation of the faithful—that is the parish visitation. The Code of Canon Law requires that the bishop or a proxy visit all parishes in the diocese over a five-year period (c. 396.1).

Of course, structures for consultation are not limited to these canonical provisions. In many dioceses one finds various boards and commissions created to oversee important dimensions of the church's ministry and mission, and many of these boards and commissions have significant lay representation. Still, one has the impression that consultation is something more of pragmatic value than a theological or even doctrinal imperative. Again, as we shall see in chapter 6, recent statements by Pope Francis offer hope that a new phase of ecclesial implementation of the council's teaching in this regard may finally be at hand.

[10] Quoted in Thomas J. Healey, "A Blueprint for Change," *America* 193, no. 8 (September 26, 2005): 15.

[11] Sharon Euart, "Structures for Participation in the Church," *Origins* 35 (May 26, 2005): 18–25. The treatment of the canonical structures for the consultation of the faithful in this section is largely drawn from Sr. Euart's address.

Toward a Noncompetitive Theology of the Relationship between Baptismal Charisms and Church Office

A third instance of the council's noncompetitive ecclesiology concerns the relationship between the ministry of the ordained and the exercise of charisms received by all believers at baptism. The years immediately before Vatican II had seen a great burst of activity on the part of the laity that often found its form in what came to be known as Catholic Action. In 1927, Pope Pius XI characterized this initiative as "the participation of the laity in the apostolate of the hierarchy." In spite of the real contributions of the many Catholic Action initiatives, we see the same problematic way of imagining the ministry and other forms of ecclesial life. To the clergy alone belonged the prerogative of actively furthering the work of the church. The laity could only do so as a kind of auxiliary to the clergy. But was there a way to conceive of lay activity in the church and in the world as something other than a participation in an apostolate that was actually proper to the ordained? Was there a way of characterizing lay activity in the church in a noncompetitive relationship with the ministry of the ordained?

The solution came, once again, by way of the council's recovery of the pneumatological conditioning of the church and its appropriation of the biblical understanding of charism.[12] The council taught that the Spirit "guides the church in the way of all truth and, uniting it in fellowship and ministry, bestows upon it different hierarchic and charismatic gifts, and in this way directs it and adorns it with his fruits" (LG 4). In this passage, "hierarchic gifts" refers to stable church office and "charismatic gifts" refers to those many charisms that the Spirit distributes among all the faithful. In council teaching, charism and office are not opposed to one another since both have the Spirit as their origin. The council was effectively acknowledging that that the Holy Spirit was coinstituting, with Christ, both institutional and charismatic elements in the church. In this way it affirmed both that church office could not function properly un-

---

[12] Congar writes: "One of the most important ways in which the holy Spirit has been restored to the pneumatological ecclesiology of the Council was in the sphere of charisms." Congar, "The Pneumatology of Vatican II," in *I Believe in the Holy Spirit*, 1:170.

less it was informed by the Holy Spirit and that charisms could not survive unless they submitted to an ordering which sought the good of the whole church.

The council successfully transcended any competition between charism and office by stressing their mutual dependence on the power of the Holy Spirit in the life of the church. For example, in several passages, the council suggested a possible theology of ordained pastoral leadership within a community animated by many charisms. Ordained pastoral leadership need not compete with the exercise of the many gifts of the faithful. Each requires the other. According to conciliar teaching, those ordained to pastoral leadership were not to absorb into their own ministry all the tasks proper to building up the church. Rather, the church's pastors were exhorted to recognize, empower, and affirm the gifts of all God's people. In *Lumen Gentium*, the council taught:

> Allotting his gifts "at will to each individual," he [the holy Spirit] also distributes special graces among the faithful of every rank. By these gifts, he makes them fit and ready to undertake various tasks and offices for the renewal and building up of the church. . . . Whether these charisms be very remarkable or more simple and widely diffused, they are to be received with thanksgiving and consolation since they are primarily suited to and useful for the needs of the church. . . . Those who have charge over the church should judge the genuineness and orderly use of these gifts, and it is especially their office not indeed to extinguish the Spirit, but to test all things and hold fast to what is good. (LG 12, see also AA 3)

The Decree on Priestly Ministry and Life likewise asserted the responsibility of the priest to affirm and nurture the gifts of the faithful: "While testing the spirits to discover if they be of God, they must discover with faith, recognize with joy, and foster diligently the many and varied charismatic gifts of the laity, whether these be of a humble or more exalted kind" (PO 9). These passages situated ordained pastoral ministry not above but within the Christian community. The ordained minister is responsible for the discernment and coordination of the charisms and ministries of all the baptized.

The council insisted on the right and obligation of the faithful to use the charisms given them by the Spirit for service in the church and in the world.[13] The full significance of this development depends here on a noncompetitive conception of ecclesial power. As we saw in our treatment of the pope/bishop relationship, a competitive theology of power inevitably sees power as a possession held by some at the expense of others. Moreover, a competitive theology of ecclesial power tends to argue for such power as the exclusive province of the ordained. This competitive theology is reflected in the influential "German school" of canon law that locates ecclesiastical power exclusively with the ordained. This preoccupation with the distribution of ecclesiastical power is a stubborn remnant of the more competitive, juridical ecclesiology typical of the hierocratic form of the church. The council nudged the church toward a new theological vision, one that insisted that the pastors do not compete with the charisms of the baptized but lead the church by testing, empowering, and ordering those charisms for the building up of the church and in service of its mission.

This noncompetitive account of the relationship between the ministry of the ordained and the exercise of the gifts of the baptized is in fact ritually enacted in the celebration of the Eucharist. As Massimo Faggioli has persuasively argued, one finds in the first text considered by the council, its liturgy constitution, an ecclesiology that has been too easily dismissed as but an early and more primitive version of the more "mature" ecclesiology of later council documents.[14] Faggioli insists that considerations of *Sacrosanctum Concilium* not be limited to the proper implementation of liturgical reform; this document contains, in germ, a compelling ecclesial vision, one only partially followed in the council's subsequent documents.

In article 2 of *Sacrosanctum Concilium*, the council asserted that the Eucharist "is supremely effective in enabling the faithful to express in their lives and portray to others the mystery of Christ and *the real nature of the true church*." It is in the liturgy that the deepest reality of the church is manifested. Consequently, while the church

[13] According to John Beal, this "is the only right asserted in the documents of Vatican II not incorporated into the revised code." John Beal, "It Shall Not Be So Among You: Crisis in the Church: Crisis in Church Law," in *Governance, Accountability and the Future of the Catholic Church*, ed. Francis Oakley and Bruce Russett (New York: Continuum, 2004), 97.

[14] Massimo Faggioli, *True Reform: Liturgy and Ecclesiology in* Sacrosanctum Concilium (Collegeville, MN: Liturgical Press, 2012).

is not church solely when it gathers in the eucharistic *synaxis*, the council understood that "the liturgy is the summit *toward which* the activity of the church is directed; it is also the source *from which* all its power flows (SC 10)." This suggests that a renewed vision of the church could, and should, be read off of the corporate worship of the whole people of God.

In the first chapter of the liturgy constitution, under the "The Reform of the Liturgy," we find a subsection titled "Norms Drawn from the Hierarchic and Communal Nature of the Liturgy." Though it does not appear in the text itself, this title introduces a formulation that will appear in later conciliar texts,[15] namely, the assertion of the importance of being in *communio hierarchica*, "hierarchical communion," with the pope and bishops. Here we encounter a direct response to the excesses of the hierocratic form of the church for while the language of "hierarchy" is retained, it is also thoroughly reimagined within a liturgical framework.

The difficulty with the language of hierarchical communion is that one easily ends up simply reinforcing the hierocratic, pyramidal view of the church that is so central to the church's long-standing hierocratic form. As we saw in the first chapter, this descending chain-of-command view of hierarchy has persisted in certain sectors of the church, in spite of the council's reforms, up to the present. Feminist theologians have rightly challenged this pyramidal understanding of "hierarchy" as one of the many concepts employed in the church to subordinate the laity in general and women in particular.[16] Some theologians argue that the term "hierarchical" can be retained if we purge it of those pyramidal and patriarchal conceptions.[17] When the Constitution on the Sacred Liturgy refers to the "hierarchic and

---

[15] LG 21, 22; CD 4, 5; PO 7. It appears a sixth time in 2 of *Nota Praevia*.

[16] Elisabeth Schüssler Fiorenza, *Discipleship of Equals: A Critical Feminist Ekklesia-logy of Liberation* (New York: Crossroad, 1993); Natalie Watson, *Introducing Feminist Ecclesiology* (Eugene, OR: Wipf & Stock, 2008); Mary Ann Hinsdale, "A Feminist Reflection on Postconciliar Catholic Ecclesiology," in *A Church with Open Doors: Catholic Ecclesiology for the Third Millennium*, ed. Richard R. Gaillardetz and Edward P. Hahnenberg (Collegeville, MN: Liturgical Press, 2015), 112–37.

[17] For one attempt to retrieve the notion of "hierarchy" by distinguishing between "command hierarchy" and "participatory hierarchy," see Terence L.

communal nature of the liturgy" it is not invoking a pyramidal ecclesiology. The liturgy can be said to be hierarchical, not in the sense of a
chain of command or a pyramidal structure, but in the sense that the
liturgy manifests the church as an *ordered* communion with a great
diversity of ministries and Christian activities that together build
up the life of the church.[18] The church of Jesus Christ, animated by
the Spirit, is now and has always been subject to church ordering as
it receives its life from the God who, in Christian faith, is ordered
in eternal self-giving as a triune communion of persons.

The most fundamental ordering of the church occurs in Christian initiation. This conviction is reflected in the council's call for a
thoroughgoing reform of its initiatory rites, including the restoration
of the catechumenate for adults, the revision of the baptismal rite
for infants, and the reconsideration of the rites of confirmation (SC
64–71). These calls for ritual reform were in keeping with the larger
agenda of the council often captured in the French term *ressourcement*, a "return to the sources." In this case, the council was reaching back to a more biblical vision of Christian initiation. Indeed, the
early church's theology of baptism might be thought of as the first
Christian ecclesiology.[19]

From a biblical perspective, Christian initiation "orders" or, if you
prefer, "configures" the believer to Christ *within* the community of
faith, Christ's body. Christian initiation does not just make one a different kind of individual, it draws the believer into a profound ecclesial relationship, one's ecclesial *ordo* within the life of the church.[20]
The distinctive character of this baptismally ordered relationship

---

Nichols, *That All May Be One: Hierarchy and Participation in the Church*
(Collegeville, MN: Liturgical Press, 1997).

[18] This view of the church as an ordered communion parallels in some ways
Lafont's presentation of the postconciliar church as a "structured communion."
See his *Imagining the Catholic Church: Structured Communion in the Spirit*
(Collegeville, MN: Liturgical Press, 2000).

[19] Gerard Austin, "Restoring Equilibrium after the Struggle with Heresy," in
Source and Summit: Commemorating Josef A. Jungmann, S.J., ed. Joanne M.
Pierce and Michael Downey (Collegeville, MN: Liturgical Press, 1999), 35–47 at 37.

[20] See Richard R. Gaillardetz, "The Ecclesiological Foundations of Ministry
within an Ordered Communion," in *Ordering of the Baptismal Priesthood*, ed.
Susan Wood (Collegeville, MN: Liturgical Press, 2003), 26–51.

unfolds in three dimensions. Vertically, if you will, we are baptized into communion with God, in Christ, by the power of the Spirit. Yet this relation is inseparable from our horizontal relationship with all our brothers and sisters in baptism who constitute together a communion of believers. These two dimensions of the baptismal ordering must, in turn, be conjoined to a third dimension, the movement outward toward the world in mission. This three-dimensional ecclesial relation established by Christian initiation offers us our primal identity as Christian believers and it can never be abandoned. It constitutes the very essence of Christian discipleship.

If baptism constitutes the most fundamental ordering of the people of God, in the Catholic Church we believe that some among the baptized are further ordered or reconfigured for leadership in the sacrament of holy orders. According to the council, the fullness of orders is conferred on the bishop. One of the most overlooked contributions of the liturgy constitution is its placement of the bishop at the center of the liturgical life of the diocese. The council asserted, moreover, that the most profound manifestation of the local church was encountered at diocesan liturgies presided over by the bishop (SC 41).

Regrettably, the council did not explore the full implications of defining the ministry of the bishop in terms of his eucharistic presidency. In the liturgy, the bishop is placed in a relationship of reciprocity with the gathered assembly. As presider, the bishop gathers the people of God together for corporate worship, proclaims the Scriptures, receives the gifts of bread and wine from the people, offers them up to God for and with the people, and then returns these gifts to the people, now transformed into the Bread of Life and Cup of Salvation. At no point in the liturgy does the Eucharist ever become the bishop's own private work; even as he engages in his unique presidential ministry, the bishop remains in communion with his people. Moreover, in his eucharistic presidency the mutual exchange of gifts includes not only bread and wine but also the very faith of the church. In other words, along with bread and wine, the very faith of the people is offered to the bishop, and that faith, articulated in the ongoing tradition of the church, is returned by the bishop to the people in his teaching and preaching. This new gift exchange reminds us that the faith which the bishop is ordained to safeguard is nothing other than the faith he has received from the people. The reciprocal relationship between bishop and people enacted in the liturgy opens up an understanding of not only the bishop's sacramental ministry but also his ministries of teaching and governance as well. It presents the bishop not as a dispenser of truth and grace but as the one who offers to God not only the eucharistic elements but also the faith and life of those he serves. The ministry of the bishop cannot be understood in isolation; it is only fully apprehended in the context of the church at prayer.

According to Vatican II, the priest shares and collaborates in the bishop's ministry of apostolic oversight or *episkope*. This is why the presbyter presides over any Eucharist in which the bishop is not present. The council chose not to define the bishop in terms of the priest, as had been the custom for much of the second millennium; rather, the council defined the ministry of the presbyter in terms of the bishop. The presbyter collaborates and extends the ministry of apostolic oversight entrusted to the bishop. Consequently, I would argue that the fullest theology of the presbyterate is also developed in terms of the presbyter's eucharistic presidency. In the Eucharist, the presbyter's role as liturgical president is a ritual enactment of his pastoral ministry of apostolic oversight.

Let us turn now to another ecclesial contribution of the constitution on the liturgy. In a passage that now seems so tame and obvious, the council also wrote that "servers, readers, commentators, and members of the choir also *exercise a genuine liturgical ministry*" (SC 29, emphasis mine). This passage would not even merit comment were it not for a consistent trend in recent Vatican pronouncements to obsess over the distinctiveness of the sacred ministry of the ordained. I have in mind not only the revised General Instruction on the Roman Missal and its preoccupation with the predicate "sacred," nor the document on liturgical abuses, *Redemptionis Sacramentum*, but also the 1997 interdicasterial document, "Certain Questions Regarding Collaboration of the Lay Faithful in Ministry of Priests."[21] The sense one gets in documents such as these is that the only way to enhance the dignity of the ordained is to build an ontological wall between the ordained and all other ministers of the church.

---

[21] "Some Questions Regarding Collaboration of Nonordained Faithful in Priests' Sacred Ministry," *Origins* 27 (November 27, 1997): 397–410.

How far removed this seems from the intention of the council fathers! There is no competition in the life of public service on behalf of the church. Lectors, eucharistic ministers, ministers of hospitality, deacons, priests, and bishops—these ministries do not compete with one another in the liturgy but cooperate in a wonderful way to build up the body of Christ at worship.

This sense of liturgical cooperation logically extends, as well, to all ecclesial ministries. What distinguishes the bishop from the priest from the deacon from the lector is not the question of power. A liturgical ecclesiology does not begin with what unique powers the bishop has but the priest doesn't, or what power the priest has that the deacon doesn't. Liturgical ecclesiology begins with the unique ministerial relationship of the bishop that cannot be replaced by the deacon or lector but is not for that reason intrinsically superior to the deacon or lector. The liturgy establishes ministries according to a diversity of ministerial relations that stand in an intrinsically noncompetitive relationship, not according to a descending hierarchy of ministerial powers. Anyone familiar with the conduct of relationships within your typical diocesan chancery or parish pastoral team can assure you that we are far from realizing the respectful mutuality and noncompetitive character of ministerial relationships enacted in each liturgical celebration.

Toward a Noncompetitive Theology of the Spheres of Christian Activity

This final instance of the council's shift from a competitive to a noncompetitive ecclesiology is rooted in the council's theology of mission. Yet again, the council's trinitarian framework plays an essential role in its understanding of the church's mission: "The pilgrim church is of its very nature missionary, since it draws its origin from the mission of the Son and the mission of the Holy Spirit, in accordance with the plan of God the Father" (AG 2).[22] Just as the missions of Word and Spirit establish God as fundamentally God-with-us, that is, God reaching out to all creation in order to redeem it and draw it into saving communion, so too the church is described as

---

[22] This translation is taken from Tanner.

essentially missionary. The church's mission to the world is not a dimension that is superadded to an essentialist account of the church's nature (something that is sometimes suggested when the theological phrase "the nature and mission of the church" is employed); rather the church's nature *is* to be in mission. In *Gaudium et Spes*, the council teaches that "in virtue of its mission to enlighten the whole world with the message of the Gospel and to gather together in one spirit all women and men of every nation, race and culture, the church shows itself as a sign of that amity which renders possible sincere dialogue and strengthens it" (GS 92).

The council largely eschewed that antagonistic attitude toward the world that was cultivated over centuries in response to a series of perceived threats: Protestantism, the rise of modern science, the Enlightenment, communism, and capitalism. This new missionary stance is evident in a passage from the Decree on the Apostolate of the Laity where a careful distinction, but not separation, is articulated regarding the relationship between the temporal and spiritual orders:

> The mission of the church, consequently, is not only to bring people the message and grace of Christ but also to permeate and improve the whole range of temporal things. The laity, carrying out this mission of the church, exercise their apostolate therefore in the world as well as in the church, in the temporal order as well as in the spiritual. These orders are distinct; they are nevertheless so closely linked that God's plan is, in Christ, to take the whole world up again and make of it a new creation, initially here on earth, totally at the end of time. (AA 5)

The missionary framework for grasping the relationship between the temporal and spiritual orders is further developed in both *Ad Gentes* and *Gaudium et Spes*. The latter document rejected the competitive juxtaposition of church and world in favor of a noncompetitive view of the church sent in mission into the world, a church active within the world, offering to the world the Christian Gospel while also receiving wisdom and insight from worldly realities (GS 44). Church and world were no longer conceived of as two completely different realms but overlapping and intertwined spheres of life for the baptized.

Of course this noncompetitive conception of the church/world relation was not maintained consistently throughout the council documents. This is evident in the council's inconsistent treatment of the laity. According to the Italian theologian Giovanni Magnani, one can identify in the documents two different theologies of the laity.[23] The first, which he refers to as a "contrastive" theology, tries to define the laity in contrast to the clergy and puts more emphasis on the distinctively secular character of the lay vocation. We find in *Lumen Gentium* 31 the following claim,

> To be secular is the special characteristic of the laity. . . . It is the special vocation of the laity to seek the kingdom of God by engaging in temporal affairs and directing them according to God's will. They live in the world, in each and every one of the world's occupations and callings and in the ordinary circumstances of social and family life which, as it were, form the context of their existence. (LG 31)

This contrastive view presumes a more pronounced distinction between church and world as distinct spheres of Christian activity, encouraging the view that the proper province of the clergy is ecclesiastical activity in the church while the realization of the laity's proper vocation lies in the secular order. Although called to a more active participation in the mission of the church, the laity nevertheless realize what is truly proper to their Christian vocation in the temporal order. This contrastive theology of the laity was unable to escape a more competitive conception of church and world.

Edward Schillebeeckx criticized this theological trajectory, claiming that in spite of its significant advances, it still started from largely "hierarchological premises" that reflected, using the terminology of this article, a competitive relationship between clergy and laity and a correlative competitive relationship between church and world:

> Here it was often forgotten that this positive content [of a "theology of the laity"] is already provided by the Christian content of the word *christifidelis*. The characteristic feature of the laity began to be explained as their relation to the world, while the characteristic of the clergy was their relationship to the church. Here both sides failed to do justice to the ecclesial dimension of any *christifidelis* and his or her

---

[23] Giovanni Magnani, "Does the So-Called Theology of the Laity Possess a Theological Status?," in *Vatican II: Assessment and Perspectives*, vol. 1, ed. René Latourelle (New York: Paulist Press, 1988), 597ff.

relationship to the world. The clergy become the apolitical men of the church; the laity are the less ecclesially committed, politically involved "men of the world." In this view, the ontological status of the "new humanity" reborn with the baptism of the Spirit was not recognized in his or her own individual worth, but only from the standpoint of the status of the clergy.[24]

Although there is no denying that traces of this competitive schematization of the lay vocation can be found in select council texts, a deeper and more theologically mature conciliar impulse led in another direction. This deeper impulse situated any lay/clergy distinction within the context of an overarching "common matrix," as Kenan Osborne has referred to it.[25] The council's frequent use of the term *christifidelis* to refer to all the baptized and its appeal to the priesthood of all believers further reinforced this common matrix.

Magnani characterizes this alternative trajectory as an *intensive* theology of the laity. The life of the typical lay Christian is simply a more intensive realization of the situation of all the *christifideles*, including the ordained and consecrated religious.[26] The council was not attempting a formal definition of the laity.[27] This is confirmed in Cardinal Wright's *relatio* on behalf of the subcommission regarding *Lumen Gentium* 31 where he noted that the text should not be read as an "ontological definition" but merely as a "typological description."[28] Obviously Christians will differ in the mode of their participation in the church's mission according to their gifts, temperament, and particular vocation, but none are exempt from the church's worldly orientation. All Christians are called to participate, in ways appropri-

---

[24] Edward Schillebeeckx, *The Church with a Human Face* (New York: Crossroad, 1985), 157.

[25] Kenan B. Osborne, *Ministry: Lay Ministry in the Roman Catholic Church* (New York: Paulist Press, 1993), 530ff.

[26] Magnani, "Does the So-Called Theology of the Laity Possess a Theological Status?," 611.

[27] Ibid., 604–20.

[28] *Acta Synodalia* 3/1, 282. This also appeared in the *relatio* introducing chapter 4, see *Acta Synodalia* 3/3, 62. For one interpretation of this distinction see Edward Schillebeeckx, "The Typological Definition of the Christian Layman according to Vatican II," in *The Mission of the Church* (New York: Seabury Press, 1973), 90–116.

ate to their ecclesial station, in the church's mission. By establishing the foundational character of baptism, discipleship, and our shared obligations for Christian mission the council did much to nudge the church toward a more noncompetitive theology that refuses to place church and world as two competing spheres of Christian activity.

In this chapter I have proposed that the council's recovery of a theology of the Holy Spirit played a central role in enabling the council to transcend competitive ecclesiological relations. The four ecclesiological relations that I offered here by no means exhaust the council's noncompetitive framework. This analysis might easily be extended to other topics in conciliar teaching, including the Catholic Church's relationship to other Christian churches and ecclesial communities as well as Christianity's relationship to other non-Christian religions. The four topics explored here, however, are sufficient, I hope, to demonstrate the fruitfulness of this interpretation of conciliar teaching. Seeing the council's work as a shift from a competitive to a noncompetitive theology of the church can provide a more coherent rendering of the council's enduring contributions and help the church today articulate a new agenda for ecclesial reform capable of furthering the council's vision.

6

Pope Francis and the Reception of Vatican II

In this chapter we explore a different kind of synthetic reading of the council, one currently enacted in the pontificate of Pope Francis. The church's first Jesuit pope and first Latin American pope is offering the church a fresh reception of the council, one that holds promise for continuing the unfinished building project of Vatican II. Francis's four most recent predecessors were all participants at the council. Of the four, Paul VI, St. John Paul II, and Benedict XVI each carried forward distinct elements of conciliar teaching. At the same time, significant conciliar themes were either neglected entirely or given only a cursory nod. Although Pope Francis was not ordained a priest until four years after the council's close, his biographer Austen Ivereigh contends: "The Council would be Bergoglio's greatest teacher, and the single greatest source, later, of his pontificate."[1] This pope has boldly returned to the foreground a number of those neglected conciliar teachings. By carrying forward multiple conciliar contributions, he has also made possible a greater appreciation of their profound intersections.

[1] Austen Ivereigh, *The Great Reformer: Francis and the Making of a Radical Pope* (New York: Henry Holt and Co., 2014), 57.

I: The Missiological Vision of Vatican II—
A Centrifugal Church

Pope Francis calls for a church sent in mission as a sign and in-strument of God's mercy and justice. His ready appropriation of the language of the "new evangelization," so central to both John Paul II and Benedict XVI, highlights an undeniable continuity between Francis and his predecessors. The pope speaks of the new evangeli-zation fourteen times in *Evangelii Gaudium*.[2] Nevertheless, one can detect in his writing a subtle modulation of his predecessors' theology of mission. This modulation is reflected in his preference for the language of "missionary discipleship." We can trace this term back to CELAM's 2007 Aparecida document that then-Cardinal Bergoglio helped write. Francis uses the term to stress the fundamentally cen-trifugal thrust of the church's activity and the need for Christians to enter into a deeper and more profound solidarity with the world. As is familiar to anyone who has been paying any attention to Francis, one of his favorite expressions is the "smell of the sheep." He has used this image in an address to newly appointed bishops, calling for them to have the smell of the sheep on them.[3] He appealed to it in a homily at a priestly ordination,[4] and in *Evangelii Gaudium* he applies it to all the baptized, precisely in their work as missionaries:

> An evangelizing community gets involved by word and deed in people's daily lives; it bridges distances, it is willing to abase itself if necessary, and it embraces human life, touching the suffering flesh of Christ in others. Evangelizers thus take on the "smell of the sheep" and the sheep are willing to hear their voice. An evangelizing community is also supportive, standing by people at every step of the way, no matter how difficult or lengthy this may prove to be. (EG 24)

---

[2] All references to *Evangelii Gaudium* will be made parenthetically in the body of this work and denoted as "EG" followed by the article number. The English translation may be accessed online at http://w2.vatican.va/content /francesco/en/apost_exhortations/documents/papa-francesco_esortazione-ap _20131124_evangelii-gaudium.html.

[3] Francis, "Address to a Group of Newly Appointed Bishops Taking Part in a Conference, 19 September 2013," in *The Church of Mercy: A Vision for the Church* (Chicago: Loyola Press, 2014), 85–88.

[4] Francis, "Homily, 21 April 2013," in *The Church of Mercy*, 89–95.

For Pope Francis, the church's mission begins not with strident condemnation but with an openness to "a peaceful and multifaceted culture of encounter" (EG 220). He certainly is not blind to the brokenness of the world. This is, after all, a pope who has issued stringent denunciations of the evils of capitalist excess and its attendant "throw away culture" (EG 53). He is also aware of the dangers and challenges peculiar to our postmodern world, yet there is less emphasis on decrying the evils of secularism or the "tyranny of relativism" than was the case with his predecessor. The missionary encounter that Francis envisions has two aspects. First, the church must be willing to encounter the world on its own turf, with humility and openness. Second, the missionary encounter must be, in the end, an encounter with Christ. In the midst of an enormously original and innovative program for ecclesial renewal, the robust Christocentrism that governs his theology of mission stands in continuity with his predecessor. Indeed, in *Evangelii Gaudium* he directly quotes Pope Benedict: "Being a Christian is not the result of an ethical choice or a lofty idea, but the encounter with an event, a person, which gives life a new horizon and a decisive direction" (EG 7). Nevertheless, his emphasis on the centrifugal impetus of the church marks an orientation that was not nearly as pronounced with Pope Benedict.

The centrifugal orientation of the church requires that Christians "go forth to everyone without exception" (EG 48). He writes: "I prefer a Church which is bruised, hurting and dirty because it has been out on the streets, rather than a Church which is unhealthy from being confined and from clinging to its own security" (EG 49). We need, he insists, a church "that knows how to open her arms and welcome everyone."[5] One can see here once again the influence of Latin American theology. Within days of his papal election, Francis began speaking of his preference for "a church of and for the poor." Christians must vacate any space that keeps them secure and buffered against the reality of poverty. We must be attentive to the "cry of the poor." This means working to address the causes of poverty and injustice in our world but it also requires a deep solidarity with the poor. In *Evangelii Gaudium* he writes:

---

[5] Francis, "General Audience, 2 October, 2013," in *The Church of Mercy*, 31.

> The word "solidarity" is a little worn and at times poorly understood,
> but it refers to something more than a few sporadic acts of generosity.
> It presumes the creation of a new mindset which thinks in terms of
> community and the priority of the life of all over the appropriation of
> goods by a few. (EG 188)

This new mind-set goes to the heart of the pope's sense of the church.
The church does not merely address the needs of the poor, it must
learn from them, from their participation in the *sensus fidei* in which
they teach us of the suffering Christ (EG 198). He evokes the image
of the church as a "field hospital" that goes out to meet the wounded
on the battlefield of life: "It is useless to ask a seriously injured person
if he has high cholesterol and about the level of his blood sugars! You
have to heal his wounds."[6]

At every step of the way, the missionary church must show the
world the face of mercy. This stress on mission and mercy has given
Pope Francis's eucharistic theology a distinctive character, one that
distinguishes him from his predecessor. He writes:

> Everyone can share in some way in the life of the Church; everyone can
> be part of the community, nor should the doors of the sacraments be
> closed for simply any reason. This is especially true of the sacrament
> which is itself "the door": baptism. The Eucharist, although it is the
> fullness of sacramental life, is not a prize for the perfect but a powerful
> medicine and nourishment for the weak. These convictions have pas-
> toral consequences that we are called to consider with prudence and
> boldness. Frequently, we act as arbiters of grace rather than its facilita-
> tors. But the Church is not a tollhouse; it is the house of the Father,
> where there is a place for everyone, with all their problems. (EG 47)

Pope Francis's commitment to a centrifugal church fundamentally
oriented toward mission is further explored in his frequent juxtaposition of "center" and "periphery," an insight he likely gained from
Yves Congar. For Congar, the place where creative ecclesial initiative

---

[6] Antonio Spadaro, "A Big Heart Open to God: The Exclusive Interview with
Pope Francis," trans. Massimo Faggioli, Sarah Christopher Faggioli, Dominic
Robinson, Patrick Howell, and Griffin Oleynick, *America* 209, no. 8 (September
30, 2013), available at http://americamagazine.org/pope-interview.

occurs is rarely at the center of the church but rather at the periphery. In *True and False Reform in the Church*, Congar writes:

> Initiatives often start at the periphery. They say that history develops at its margins and that's right. The margin is closer to the periphery than to the center. Further, the center, with its vocation to oversee *structure*, prefers something *defined* to something that is searching and striving for expression. Yet a spiritual organism is more likely to grow out of the elements searching and striving for expression.[7]

Pope Francis, I believe, has expanded on Congar's appeal to the ecclesial significance of the periphery.[8] The pope has been critical of a church content to abide in static and self-contained ecclesial structures. In an address to the bishops of Brazil, he insisted that authentic missionary discipleship will inevitably lead Christians "away from the center and toward the peripheries."[9]

Francis is not a professional theologian, and he has only occasionally addressed the role of the theologian in the church. In his December 6, 2013, address to the International Theological Commission, however, he situates the work of theology at the heart of this missionary encounter:

> Theologians, then, are "pioneers . . . in the Church's dialogue with cultures. But being pioneers is important also because sometimes we think they [theologians] stay back, stay in the barracks. . . . No, they are on the frontier! This dialogue of the Church with cultures is a dialogue at once critical and benevolent, which must foster the reception

---

[7] See Yves Congar, *True and False Reform in the Church* (Collegeville, MN: Liturgical Press, 2011), 240. See also Congar, "Theology of the Council," *American Ecclesiastical Review* 155 (1966): 220–21. Paul Philibert offers a helpful distillation of Congar's use of the relationship between "center" and "periphery" in his article "When Not in Rome: Lessons from the Periphery of the Church, *America* 210, no. 10 (March 24, 2014), available online at http://americamagazine.org/issue/when-not-rome.

[8] The frequent reference to Congar is not accidental. Austen Ivereigh writes: "His [Francis's] lodestars have been two French theologians, Yves Congar and Henri de Lubac, who taught him how to unite God's People by a radical reform that will lead them to holiness." Ivereigh, *The Great Reformer*, xv.

[9] Quoted in John L. Allen, Jr., *Against the Tide: The Radical Leadership of Pope Francis* (Liguori, MO: Liguori Publications, 2014), 47.

of the Word of God by people "from every nation, from all tribes and peoples and tongues" (Rev 7:9).[10]

According to Francis, the theologian must exercise her or his vocation at the periphery as well, working on the front lines of the church's missionary engagement with the world today.

Francis also calls for a movement from the center to the periphery in his reflections on religious life. In November 2013 he engaged in a lively exchange at a gathering of the superiors of male religious orders. At that meeting he boldly challenged those in religious life:

> Being at the periphery helps to see and to understand better, to ana-
> lyze reality more correctly, to shun centralism and ideological ap-
> proaches. . . . This is really very important to me: the need to become
> acquainted with reality by experience, to spend time walking on the
> periphery in order really to become acquainted with the reality and life-
> experiences of people. If this does not happen we then run the risk of
> being abstract ideologists or fundamentalists, which is not healthy.[11]

It is from the periphery that vowed religious are best positioned to exercise the prophetic character of their vocation:

> In the church, the religious are called to be prophets in particular by
> demonstrating how Jesus lived on this earth, and to proclaim how the
> kingdom of God will be in its perfection. A religious must never give
> up prophecy. This does not mean opposing the hierarchical part of the
> church, although the prophetic function and the hierarchical structure
> do not coincide. I am talking about a proposal that is always positive,
> but it should not cause timidity.[12]

Francis recognizes that professed religious can be in communion with the hierarchy without being subsumed into it.

---

[10] Francis, "Address to the International Theological Commission, December 6, 2013." This address is available online at http://www.vatican.va/holy_father/francesco/speeches/2013/december/documents/papa-francesco_20131206_commissione-teologica_en.html.

[11] Francis, " 'Wake up the World!' Conversation with Pope Francis about Religious Life," ed. Antonio Spadaro, *La Civilta Cattolica* (2014) 1:3–17, available at http://www.laciviltacattolica.it/articoli_download/extra/Wake_up_the_world.pdf.

[12] Spadaro, "A Big Heart Open to God."

Let me conclude this section with a brief reflection on the relationship between church mission and church reform. Pope Francis does not see commitments to church mission and structural reform as mutually exclusive alternatives. In fact, for Francis, one is the necessary precondition for the other. In his July 2013 address to the coordinating committee of CELAM during his visit to Brazil, he said:

> The "change of structures" (from obsolete ones to new ones) will not be the result of reviewing an organizational flow chart, which would lead to a static reorganization; rather it will result from the very dynamics of mission. What makes obsolete structures pass away, what leads to a change of heart in Christians, is precisely missionary spirit.[13]

He further develops this idea in *Evangelii Gaudium:*

> I dream of a "missionary option," that is, a missionary impulse capable of transforming everything, so that the Church's customs, ways of doing things, times and schedules, language and structures can be suitably channeled for the evangelization of today's world rather than for her self-preservation. The renewal of structures demanded by pastoral conversion can only be understood in this light: as part of an effort to make them more mission-oriented, to make ordinary pastoral activity on every level more inclusive and open, to inspire in pastoral workers a constant desire to go forth and in this way to elicit a positive response from all those whom Jesus summons to friendship with himself. (EG 27)

This commitment to a program of ecclesial reform in service of the church's mission has led the pope to criticize a more bureaucratic way of dealing with pastoral issues (EG 63). He has complained that "the church sometimes has locked itself up in small things, in small-minded rules." All of this suggests that proposals for church reform are not to be evaluated in relation to their employment of secular categories or by the extent to which they threaten the status

---

[13] Francis, "July 2013 Address to the Coordinating Committee of CELAM." This address is available online at http://www.vatican.va/holy_father/francesco /speeches/2013/july/documents/papa-francesco_20130728_gmg-celam-rio _en.html.

quo but rather by their effectiveness in facilitating the church's mission in the world.

II: A Listening Church

A second feature of Francis's emerging ecclesiological vision is his call for a "listening church." Francis speaks positively about a church that will be messy precisely because of its commitment to honest dialogue, listening, and even disagreement. In his interview, "A Big Heart Open to God," he reflects on the meaning of *sentire cum ecclesiae*. "Thinking with the church" requires, first of all, that we get beyond our own self-styled, and often self-serving, credos. There is much to be mined here in the light of recent studies on the deregulation and commodification of religion and the perils this represents for the experience of religious community. Yet for Francis, "thinking with the church" also means much more than a scrupulous, servile obedience to every ecclesiastical decree. It means thinking with the *whole* church and not just the ones who count ecclesiastically. It means daring to enter into a "complex web of relationships" and living in receptive solidarity with all God's people. It means recalling not only the infallibility of the church's teachers but also, as the council taught, the infallibility of the believing church. And then there is this quite remarkable statement: "When the dialogue among the people and the bishops and the pope goes down this road and is genuine," Pope Francis contends, "then it is assisted by the Holy Spirit."[14] Let us not overlook the audacity of this claim. Francis is saying that we can be confident of the assistance of the Holy Spirit to the bishops *on the condition that* they are open to listening to others. This perspective stands in startling contrast to the almost mechanistic notions of the assistance of the Holy Spirit often invoked by church leaders. Indeed, Pope Francis's mature pneumatology is one of the more unappreciated features of his theological vision.

In Evangelii Gaudium, we come to the end of a *de facto* fifty-year papal moratorium on the council's teaching on the sense of

---

[14] Spadaro, "A Big Heart Open to God."

the faithful.[15] Francis specifically exhorts church leaders to attend
to the graced wisdom of the whole people of God. He recalls the
Second Vatican Council's teaching on the infallibility of the people
of God *in credendo.* "The presence of the Spirit gives Christians a
certain connaturality with divine realities, and a wisdom which enables them to grasp those realities intuitively, even when they lack
the wherewithal to give them precise expression" (EG 119). Francis
invokes the work of theology at precisely this juncture. In his 2013
address to the ITC, he insisted that it is the task of the theologian
"to develop criteria for discerning authentic expressions of the *sensus
fidelium."*[16] A year later, addressing the ITC once again, he would
repeat this theme, reminding the commission that "the theologian
is, above all, a believer who listens to the living Word of God and
welcomes it into his heart and mind . . . but he must also humbly
listen to what the Spirit tells the Church through the different manifestations of faith lived by the People of God."[17]

Francis has directly challenged bishops to broaden their practice
of consultation:

> In his [the bishop's] mission of fostering a dynamic, open and mission-
> ary communion, he will have to encourage and develop the means of
> participation proposed in the Code of Canon Law and other forms of
> pastoral dialogue, out of a desire to listen to everyone and not simply to
> those who would tell him what he would like to hear. Yet the principal
> aim of these participatory processes should not be ecclesiastical organi-
> zation but rather the missionary aspiration of reaching everyone. (EG 31)

What is particularly welcome in this passage is the recognition that
consultation is more than gathering together safe voices that function

---

[15] Since the publication of *Evangelii Gaudium,* the International Theological
Commission published in 2014 a quite positive document on the sense of
the faithful titled *"Sensus Fidei* in the Life of the Church." The document is
available online at http://www.vatican.va/roman_curia/congregations/cfaith/
cti_documents/rc_cti_20140610_sensus-fidei_en.html.

[16] "Address of Pope Francis to Members of the International Theological Commission, December 6, 2013," available online at http://w2.vatican.va/content
/francesco/en/speeches/2013/december/documents/papa-francesco_20131206
_commissione-teologica.html.

[17] *Vatican Information Service,* Year 22, Num. 217 (December 5, 2014).

as little more than an ecclesiastical echo chamber. I suspect that most bishops and pastors—for that matter, most university presidents, theology department chairs, and presidents of theological societies—think that they are consultative just because they seek out the opinions of others. The pope rightly insists that authentic ecclesial consultation that aspires to be more than a pragmatic public relations maneuver—that aspires, that is, to be a genuine listening to the Spirit—must attend to a wide range of voices, including those in ecclesial exile of one kind or another.

The pope's desire for a humble, listening, discerning church has led him to make regular pleas for the recovery and reform of consultative and collegial structures (e.g., episcopal synods):

> The consistories [of cardinals], the synods [of bishops] are, for example, important places to make real and active this consultation. We must, however, give them a less rigid form. I do not want token consultations, but real consultations. The consultation group of eight cardinals, this "outsider" advisory group, is not only my decision, but it is the result of the will of the cardinals, as it was expressed in the general congregations before the conclave. And I want to see that this is a real, not ceremonial consultation.[18]

We saw evidence of this in the preparation for the extraordinary synod on the family in which Cardinal Baldiserri, the secretary general of the Synod of Bishops, called for bishops to consult the faithful regarding their beliefs and concerns on the topic of marriage and family. In Francis's opening address, he exhorted the synod participants to speak frankly:

> One general and basic condition is this: speaking honestly. Let no one say: "I cannot say this, they will think this or this of me." . . . It is necessary to say with *parrhesia* all that one feels. After the last Consistory (February 2014), in which the family was discussed, a Cardinal wrote to me, saying: what a shame that several Cardinals did not have the courage to say certain things out of respect for the Pope, perhaps believing that the Pope might think something else. This is not good, this is not *synodality*, because it is necessary to say all that, in the Lord, one feels the need to say: without polite deference, without hesitation.

---

[18] Spadaro, "A Big Heart Open to God."

And, at the same time, one must listen with humility and welcome, with an open heart, what your brothers say. *Synodality* is exercised with these two approaches. For this reason I ask of you, please, to employ these approaches as brothers in the Lord: speaking with *parrhesia* and listening with humility.[19]

What followed this remarkable exhortation was a dramatic departure from the previous, curially scripted affairs. The 2014 synod was marked by a genuine exchange of viewpoints and often lively disagreement. At this writing, the church is in the midst of preparations for the fall 2015 ordinary synod on the family and all signs point to a continued emphasis on the need to listen to the insights and concerns of the ordinary Christian faithful. The pope clearly expects that, in the forthcoming synod, the bishops are not only to exchange their personal viewpoints; they must give voice to the lived experience and genuine pastoral needs and challenges of the faithful entrusted to their care.

Francis's eagerness for more effective consultative structures and concrete collegial mechanisms has led him to create an entirely new entity—the Council of Cardinals—which, as currently constituted, functions in a way not unlike the permanent synod that many of the bishops had requested at the council.[20] We must also note the way in which Pope Francis has used his papal authority to appoint members of the College of Cardinals to dramatically transform that institution. In the not too distant past, Italians dominated membership in the college, and most of its members either held high-ranking curial offices or were heads of prestigious dioceses. In his first two consistories, Pope Francis has largely ignored custom, appointing members based not on ecclesiastical precedent or rank but on a determination that this electoral body must reflect the global nature of the church, bringing neglected voices into the circle of papal advisers.

---

[19] Francis, "Opening Address of the 2014 Synod of Bishops, October 6, 2014." The text of this address is available online at http://saltandlighttv.org/blog /general/pope-francis-opening-address-of-2014-synod-of-bishops.

[20] I do not, however, want to ignore the differences. The permanent synod envisioned at the council would have been a far more representative structure with more deliberative authority than the Council of Cardinals currently possesses. There is still a need for the church to pursue the possibility of establishing a permanent synod as an expression of collegiality in service of the church.

Finally, the pope's commitment to a listening church is evident in his preference for extemporaneous interviews and informal dialogue over the promulgation of normative pronouncements. It is tempting to dismiss these interactions. We are accustomed to such a juridical conception of the magisterium that, unless papal teaching yields a formal document to which one could ascribe the proper juridical authority, we are inclined to dismiss it. But need papal teaching occur only in juridically validated forms? Might not Pope Francis be introducing a new genre of magisterial teaching, one that is more provisional and open-ended in character? The inherently dialogical and contextual character of an interview may be more in keeping with the council's commitment to ecclesial dialogue and discernment than the more familiar papal act of issuing carefully vetted ecclesiastical decrees.

III: Ecclesial Subsidiarity

Pope Francis's commitment to ecclesial subsidiarity represents the third feature of his fresh reception of Vatican II. Without ever using the term itself, the Second Vatican Council encouraged ecclesial subsidiarity in the liturgy constitution, giving to regional episcopal conferences significant authority in liturgical matters (SC 22; 36; 39–40; 44). We might define the principle of ecclesial subsidiarity as follows: *The primary responsibility for the realization of the individual Christian vocation and the fulfillment of the mission of local Christian communities lies with those individuals and local communities themselves. Only when the realization of these goals appears unattainable at the lower level and/or threatens the faith and unity of the church universal should one expect intervention from higher levels of church life.*

In 1967, the synod of bishops recommended that the principle of subsidiarity guide the process of revising the *Code of Canon Law*. Indeed, the preface to the new code explicitly affirmed the ecclesiological applicability of the principle of subsidiarity even though the principle is largely eschewed in the code itself.[21] A quite different view of eccle-

---

[21] This principle appeared in the Preface to the Latin edition, which can be accessed online at http://www.vatican.va/archive/ENG1104/__P1.HTM.

sial subsidiarity came to the fore at the 1985 Extraordinary Synod of Bishops. At a gathering of cardinals assembled for the synod, Cardinal Jean Jerome Hamer rejected the principle, insisting that the council had avoided any ecclesial application of subsidiarity.[22] At a press conference after the conclusion of the synod, Cardinal Jan Schotte also rejected the legitimacy of subsidiarity as an ecclesiological principle. Both prelates insisted that the principle was inapplicable because the church was no mere sociological reality but rather a spiritual communion and therefore not subject to the sociological rules that apply to other secular institutions.[23] This position reflected Cardinal Ratzinger's own concerns regarding the dangers of both a sociological reductionism and an ecclesiological relativism. In *Pastores Gregis*, John Paul II himself expressed reservations regarding subsidiarity.[24]

In spite of this ambivalence, many of the churches of the global south have continued to affirm the ecclesiological importance of the principle. The Federation of Asian Bishops Conferences has regularly insisted on the value of ecclesial subsidiarity, holding that pastoral decisions concerning the life of the church are best made at the local level. For the Asian church, this is not an abstract sociological axiom but a concrete principle of ecclesial action that flows from a theology of the local church.

Although Francis prefers to speak of ecclesial "decentralization," a theologically less helpful formulation in my view, there can be no doubt that this pope from the global south is effectively recovering the principle of ecclesial subsidiarity. Early in 2014, a Brazilian bishop disclosed a conversation with Francis in which he claimed

[22] The text of his address may be found in *Synode extraordinaire, Célébration de Vatican II* (Paris: Cerf, 1986), 598–604.

[23] For a review of this argument see Ad Leys, *Ecclesiological Impacts of the Principle of Subsidiarity* (Kampen, NL: Kok, 1995), 113–19; Joseph Komonchak, "Subsidiarity in the Church: The State of the Question," *The Jurist* 48 (1988): 298–349, at 336–37.

[24] John Paul II, Post-Synodal Apostolic Exhortation *Pastores Gregis*, 56, available at http://www.vatican.va/holy_father/john_paul_ii/apost_exhortations/documents/hf_jp-ii_exh_20031016_pastores-gregis_en.html. For a more developed treatment of ecclesial subsidiarity, see Richard R. Gaillardetz, *The Church in the Making*: Lumen Gentium, Christus Dominus, Orientalium Ecclesiarum (New York: Paulist Press, 2006), 80–82, 132–33.

that Francis was sympathetic to the pastoral urgency of the current priest shortage but felt that a proposal for married priests should not come from the pope but from regional episcopal conferences.[25] Although a secondhand account, the position attributed to Pope Francis is consistent with what he wrote in *Evangelii Gaudium*:

> Nor do I believe that the papal magisterium should be expected to offer a definitive or complete word on every question which affects the Church and the world. It is not advisable for the Pope to take the place of local Bishops in the discernment of every issue which arises in their territory. In this sense, I am conscious of the need to promote a sound "decentralization." (EG 16)

Later in the document he returns to this theme:

> The Second Vatican Council stated that, like the ancient patriarchal Churches, episcopal conferences are in a position "to contribute in many and fruitful ways to the concrete realization of the collegial spirit." Yet this desire has not been fully realized, since a juridical status of episcopal conferences which would see them as subjects of specific attributions, including genuine doctrinal authority, has not yet been sufficiently elaborated. Excessive centralization, rather than proving helpful, complicates the Church's life and her missionary outreach. (EG 32)

What is intriguing about this passage is the fact that Pope Francis footnotes John Paul II's *Apostolos Suos* when he refers to the insufficient elaboration of an understanding of the doctrinal authority of episcopal conferences. This appears to be a thinly veiled judgment of the theological inadequacies of that document.

If, in fact, Pope Francis is serious about papal decentralization, then this turn to ecclesial subsidiarity may represent his most profound effort at *ressourcement*. It amounts to a return to ancient ecclesial practice in which the principal instrument of authoritative church teaching was neither the papacy nor ecumenical councils but regional gatherings of bishops in synods that were convened to resolve pressing pastoral, theological, and doctrinal conflicts.

---

[25] David Gibson, "Are Married Priests Next on Francis's Agenda?," *National Catholic Reporter* (May 9–22, 2014): 12.

Pope Francis has already begun the most audacious attempt at curial reform since the current dicastery-based structure was established in the late sixteenth century. His intent, it is clear, is to (1) dramatically circumscribe Vatican financial activity and enhance transparency, (2) streamline the various congregations, councils, and tribunals, and (3) reconceive the Curia's relationship to the bishops as one of service to pope and bishops rather than supervision.

IV: The Pastoral Orientation of Doctrine

The final feature to consider in Pope Francis's ecclesiological vision is as much a matter of fundamental theology as it is of ecclesiology. What I have in mind here is the role the pope assigns to church doctrine in both mediating divine revelation and nurturing Catholic Christian identity. Pope Francis offers a balanced understanding of church doctrine that has carried forward the council's emphasis on a more kerygmatic theology of revelation, a spirit of "doctrinal humility," and a commitment to the broader pastoral orientation of church doctrine.

The dependence on the council's kerygmatic theology of revelation is obvious. In his address at the plenary session of the Congregation for the Doctrine of the Faith, Pope Francis distilled his understanding of doctrine in one sentence: "In reality, doctrine has the sole purpose of serving the life of the People of God and it seeks to assure our faith of a sure foundation."[26] This determination to ground doctrine in its relationship to a more basic Christian "foundation" reflects his retrieval of one of the most neglected themes of the council, the "hierarchy of truths." The council wrote, "When comparing doctrines with one another, they should remember that in catholic doctrine there exists an order or 'hierarchy' of truths, since they vary in their relation to the foundation of the Christian faith" (UR 11). This passage introduced a crucial distinction between the content of divine revelation, understood as God's self-communication in Christ by

---

[26] Francis, "Address to the Congregation for the Doctrine of the Faith, January 31, 2014." The text is available online at http://www.zenit.org/en/articles/pope-francis-address-to-congregation-for-the-doctrine-of-the-faith.

the power of the Spirit, and those church doctrines that, in varying degrees, mediate that content. Yet, the council was also proposing that there is a differentiation in the content mediated by various doctrines themselves; not every doctrine relates in the same way or to the same degree to the kerygmatic foundation of Christian faith.

Unfortunately, since the time of the council there has been little recourse to the hierarchy of truths in magisterial documents. In an important study of the topic, Catherine Clifford uncovers but a single papal reference to the hierarchy of truths in a major magisterial document prior to Pope Francis.[27] Pope Francis has recalled for us, however, the true spirit of this neglected teaching. He insists in *Evangelii Gaudium* that doctrines are not ends in themselves; they serve us when they draw us into life-giving relationship with Christ. He writes:

> All revealed truths derive from the same divine source and are to be believed with the same faith, yet some of them are more important for giving direct expression to the heart of the Gospel. In this basic core, what shines forth is the beauty of the saving love of God made manifest in Jesus Christ who died and rose from the dead. In this sense, the Second Vatican Council explained, "in Catholic doctrine there exists an order or a 'hierarchy' of truths, since they vary in their relation to the foundation of the Christian faith." This holds true as much for the dogmas of faith as for the whole corpus of the Church's teaching, including her moral teaching. (EG 36)

Francis understands the council's teaching on the hierarchy of truths as more than just ranking doctrines; the council wished to relate doctrine to something more basic, the Christian *kerygma*. For Francis too, doctrine is always at the service of the fundamental Christian message. This presupposes the sound insight that the language of

---

[27] Catherine Clifford, "L'herméneutique d'un principe herméneutique: La hiérarchie des vérités," in *L'Autorité et les autorités: L'herméneutique théologique de Vatican II*, ed. Gilles Routhier and Guy Jobin (Paris: Cerf, 2010), 69–91, at 70. According to Clifford, the single instance is found in John Paul II's encyclical on ecumenism, *Ut Unum Sint* (37), where it appears, however, without any developed explication or application. This document can be accessed at http://www.vatican.va/holy_father/john_paul_ii/encyclicals/documents/hf _jp-ii_enc_25051995_ut-unum-sint_en.html.

doctrine is a kind of second-order language that expresses in precise propositional terms the central convictions of the Christian faith. This more formal, propositional language, however necessary, inevitably puts doctrine at several degrees of abstraction from the Gospel as it is experienced concretely in the life of discipleship. He writes:

> Pastoral ministry in a missionary style is not obsessed with the disjointed transmission of a multitude of doctrines to be insistently imposed. When we adopt a pastoral goal and a missionary style which would actually reach everyone without exception or exclusion, the message has to concentrate on the essentials, on what is most beautiful, most grand, most appealing and at the same time most necessary. The message is simplified, while losing none of its depth and truth, and thus becomes all the more forceful and convincing. (EG 35)

Francis is not afraid to affirm church doctrine as basic to Christian identity, but he consistently orients that doctrine toward the basic Christian kerygma and situates it within the pastoral life of the church.

In Francis's still young pontificate, we already have several examples of this commitment to the pastoral orientation of doctrine. It is manifested in his openness to reconsidering the church's discipline regarding the possibility of communion for the divorced and remarried. He has no wish to reverse church doctrine on marital indissolubility *per se*, but he is committed to placing it within the field of Christian mercy. Can we recognize that there are at least some divorced and remarried couples who find themselves in a situation in which renouncing their second marriage would compound the harm caused by the failure of the first marriage and require breaking current familial commitments? In such a pastoral situation, is it not possible, he may be asking us, to find signs of grace and hope and to recognize the value of the Eucharist for such couples as "a medicine of mercy" (EG 47)?

Pope Francis deftly maintains the tension between the normative claims of church doctrine and pastoral reality, that is, the concrete situations of Christians who find themselves in particular circumstances that impose their own specific demands and obligations. He refuses to see doctrine and pastoral practice as mutually exclusive options; rather, he insists that it is possible to preserve the very tension that many wish to resolve prematurely. The temptation to artificially resolve this tension comes in several forms. In his address at the conclusion of the extraordinary synod on the family in October 2014, the pope warned against

> a temptation to hostile inflexibility, that is, wanting to close oneself within the written word, (the letter) and not allowing oneself to be surprised by God, by the God of surprises, (the spirit); within the law, within the certitude of what we know and not of what we still need to learn and to achieve. From the time of Christ, it is the temptation of the zealous, of the scrupulous, of the solicitous and of the so-called— today—"traditionalists" and also of the intellectuals.[28]

Yet, he also warned of "the temptation to neglect the *'depositum fidei'* [the deposit of faith], not thinking of themselves as guardians but as owners or masters [of it]." As the church prepares for the ordinary synod on the family in the fall of 2015, Francis calls the church to have the courage to undergo honest discernment and humble listening.

A second example of Pope Francis's commitment to the pastoral orientation of doctrine is reflected in his approach to Pope Paul VI's teaching on artificial birth regulation in *Humanae Vitae*. In an interview on March 5, 2014, he responded to a direct question about adherence to this controversial papal teaching:

> It all depends on how the text of *"Humanae Vitae"* is interpreted. Paul VI himself, towards the end, recommended to confessors much mercy and attention to concrete situations. But his genius was prophetic, as he had the courage to go against the majority, to defend moral discipline, to apply a cultural brake, to oppose present and future neo-Malthusianism. The object is not to change the doctrine, but it is a matter of going into the issue in depth and to ensure that the pastoral ministry takes into account the situations of each person and what that person can do. This will also be discussed on the path to the Synod.[29]

---

[28] This papal address is available at: https://w2.vatican.va/content/francesco /en/speeches/2014/october/documents/papa-francesco_20141018_conclusione -sinodo-dei-vescovi.html.

[29] "Pope Francis' March 5 Interview with *Corriere della Sera*," by Estefania Aguirre and Alan Holdren, Catholic News Agency. The transcript of the interview can be accessed online at http://www.catholicnewsagency.com/news /transcript-pope-francis-march-5-interview-with-corriere-della-sera/.

Later, during his visit to the Philippines, Francis again reaffirmed the teaching of Paul VI, noting again that Pope Paul was courageous to challenge the cultural preoccupation with population control. At the same time, Francis counseled confessors to "be very generous" in dealing with individual couples' pastoral situations.[30] On the plane home from that trip he insisted that fidelity to church teaching on birth control must be interpreted within the context of Vatican II's call for "responsible parenthood," and he warned that fidelity to church teaching doesn't mean that married couples should "breed like rabbits."

In these various statements and interviews, there are echoes of John XXIII's call for a deeper penetration of church doctrine and its more pastoral realization. Note that, while Pope Francis insists on fidelity to *Humanae Vitae*, there is no mention of the specific injunction that every conjugal act must be open to conception. It is unclear what his attitude is regarding this moral injunction, but his interests do not seem to align well with the "theology of the body" devotees who focus on a narrow moral analysis of the "conjugal act."[31] Instead, Francis redirects our attention to the larger prophetic thrust of the encyclical. He offers the wise acknowledgment, too often lacking among critics of *Humanae Vitae*, that Paul VI was prescient regarding the dangerous allure of a contraceptive mentality that technologizes and even commodifies human reproduction in contemporary Western culture. The reference to "neo-Malthusianism" recalls the 1968 CELAM meeting at Medellin at which the Latin American bishops not only supported a liberationist interpretation of the council but also voiced their support for *Humanae Vitae*. In the 1968 Latin American context, the promotion of artificial birth control was viewed as the attempt of a rich first-world elite to control an expanding poor population.

---

[30] John L. Allen Jr., "Pope Francis Criticizes Gay Marriage, Backs Ban on Contraception," *Crux*, http://www.cruxnow.com/church/2015/01/16/pope-francis-criticizes-gay-marriage-backs-contraception-ban/.

[31] For a perceptive reflection on the reductive dangers attendant to focusing on sex as a "conjugal act," see Maureen Mullarkey, "Killing Sex to Save It," *First Things* (December 15, 2014), accessed at: http://www.firstthings.com/blogs/mullarkey/2014/12/killing-sex-to-save-it.

Francis insists that the central values embedded in the doctrine must be applied in ways that "[take] into account the situations of each person and what that person can do." This is not a pastoral compromise regarding church teaching but an authentic interpretation of the doctrine as it relates to real human persons and the concrete narrative framework within which they must make specific moral decisions. Francis is modeling a methodology of moral discernment that broadens moral reflection beyond a narrow analysis of an act to consider the human person as a whole. It is a process of moral reflection that must always consider the larger social context of any contemplated moral action.

Finally, we can consider the pope's controversial remarks on homosexuality encapsulated in his oft quoted and just as frequently misunderstood statement, "Who am I to judge?" John Langan appeals to something very much like the pastorality of doctrine in his March 2014 article in *America*. There, Langan claimed that Pope Francis was concerned not with either a simple reaffirmation or reversal of the church's official teaching on homosexuality but rather with a deep reconsideration of the church's "stance." For Langan, "stance" is distinct from a specific doctrinal formulation. To consider the church's "stance" on an issue is a matter of "critical reflection on the tradition to clarify what strengths are to be preserved and what continuities are to be affirmed even while searching for the sources of limitations in the teaching and acknowledging the development of new questions and problems."[32] A change in stance may or may not bring about a change in church doctrine. What it does allow for is a consideration of hitherto neglected factors and insights.

For many, Langan's proposal that we focus on a change in "stance" will not go far enough. They will continue to press the question: will or will not this pope reverse this or that controversial church teaching? There is, however, an important way in which the "will he or won't he" question misconstrues how doctrine develops. It is a common misconception that doctrinal change and development occur primarily by ecclesiastical fiat. In fact, history shows that doctrine changes when pastoral contexts shift and new insights emerge such that particular doctrinal formulations no longer mediate the

---

[32] John Langan, "See the Person," *America* 210, no. 8 (March 10, 2014): 14.

saving message of God's transforming love. The gradual shift in the church's condemnation of usury offers us a classic example of what I have in mind here. That teaching was not reversed in a single papal decree. Rather, there was a gradual and halting pastoral discernment that the teaching, in its classical formulation, no longer served the central values it was intended to protect, namely, the welfare of the poor.[33] Eamon Duffy explains the more circumscribed role of papal teaching in this process: "'Definitive' papal utterances are not oracles providing new information, but adjudications at the end of a wider and longer process of doctrinal reflection, consultation, and debate, often extending over centuries."[34] Magisterial teaching should come at the end of our tradition's lively engagement with a particular question, not as a way of preempting its consideration.

Certainly, church leadership contributes to the change and development of doctrine, but its role is generally more indirect. Bishops and pastoral leaders contribute to the development of doctrine when they do what Pope Francis has been insisting on: move from the center to the periphery and see, in specific pastoral contexts, how doctrine actually "works," that is, how it contributes to bringing people into a saving encounter with God's abundant love and mercy.

I do not wish to diminish the extent to which Pope Francis's postconciliar predecessors were "popes of the council." Each consistently articulated their support of the council and each made frequent reference to conciliar teaching, often quoting conciliar texts in their own magisterial documents. Each encouraged implementation of particular aspects of conciliar teaching. However, no postconciliar pope, in my view, can match Pope Francis's comprehensive and integrated retrieval of not just one teaching or another but of the council's deeper reformist impulse. One senses in his pontificate nothing of the sometimes cramped and cautious conciliar interpretations that we encountered in the earlier pontificates. Indeed, in this chapter's

[33] See John Noonan's still-classic treatment of this in *The Scholastic Analysis of Usury* (Cambridge, MA: Harvard University Press, 1957); Noonan, *The Church That Can and Cannot Change* (Notre Dame, IN: University of Notre Dame Press, 2005).

[34] Eamon Duffy, "Who Is the Pope?," *New York Times Review of Books* (February 19, 2015), accessed at: http://www.nybooks.com/articles/archives/2015/feb/19/who-is-pope-francis/.

presentation of Francis's retrieval of four central conciliar teachings, we get a sense, as if for the first time, of the full pastoral force of the council. All seven of the conciliar pillars explored in chapter 3 are on exhibit in his thought: (1) the kerygmatic and trinitarian theology of revelation; (2) dialogical engagement; (3) the priority of baptism; (4) the theology of the Holy Spirit; (5) episcopal collegiality; (6) the missiological character of the church; (7) the pilgrim church. Indeed, Francis's audacious confidence in the work of the Spirit to renew the church recalls the equally audacious vision of Pope St. John XXIII. Whether this pontificate offers a genuine *kairos* for the church, or ends up as nothing more than a historical anomaly remains unclear. But let us pray that this new pope may bring to fruition the fervent desire of his papal kindred spirit that the council bring forth in the church a new Pentecost.

7

From a Pastoral Council to a Pastoral Renewal

In the last chapter I argued that Pope Francis has taken up the challenge of continuing the council's unfinished building project. He has done so by offering a fresh reception of council teaching. In the end, however, the challenge of church reform and renewal that the council has placed before us cannot be left in the hands of any one person, even the Bishop of Rome. If our careful reading of the council has taught us anything, it is that we are all members of the church and we all bear responsibility for its ongoing reform and renewal. My modest and admittedly partial efforts to articulate an overlapping set of synthetic conciliar readings have been directed entirely toward the support of a robust program of ecclesial reform and renewal. The vision of the church, however incomplete, that I have teased out in these chapters calls for nothing less than an ecclesial conversion as regards the church's self-understanding, policies, structure, and conduct. Unfortunately, the articulation of a comprehensive program of renewal would require a separate monograph. In a concluding chapter, I can only hope to tease out some possible avenues for church renewal that draw on the two interpretative frameworks proposed in chapters 4 and 5 and the inspiration and leadership of Pope Francis displayed in chapter 6.

The Pastoral Enactment
of the Ecclesial Virtue of Humility

Let us begin with the claim that Vatican II articulated a fundamental reimagination of the church's identity and self-understanding. I have suggested that one way to make sense of the council's shift in ecclesial orientation is in terms of the appropriation of the ecclesial virtue of humility. How might a theological account of a humble yet magnanimous church underwrite robust pastoral reform and renewal?

Consider the pastoral preoccupation today, at least in the Western church, with the fragility of Catholic identity. A number of recent demographic studies have documented the extent to which new generations of Catholics are far less likely to inherit and sustain a coherent Catholic identity from their parents.[1] The reasons are many. With high divorce rates and growing numbers of single-parent families, many children are raised in households with any number of serial caregivers. This familial instability makes it less likely that children will be raised in families with stable caregivers who will consistently model the beliefs and practices of a given religious tradition from infancy to adulthood. The causes of a more fragile sense of religious identity, however, go far beyond familial instability.

Charles Taylor has argued that, while secularity ought not to be viewed as the enemy, it has created a situation in which religious belief will appear less as a given and more as one framework among many for giving meaning to one's life.[2] A complacent Catholicism that simply assumes that its central convictions are self-evidently true and meaningful cannot hope to have any traction in such a "secular age." David Lyon writes of the postmodern "deregulation of religion" in which accepted religious authorities that once guided believers in the interpretation and appropriation of religious beliefs and values have been devalued. People see themselves as "religious

---

[1] See William V. D'Antonio, Michelle Dillon, and Mary L. Gauthier, *American Catholics in Transition* (Lanham, MD: Rowman and Littlefield, 2013); Christian Smith, Kyle Longest, Jonathan Hill, and Kari Christoffersen, *Young Catholic America: Emerging Adults In, Out of, and Gone from the Church* (New York: Oxford University Press, 2014).

[2] Charles Taylor, *A Secular Age* (Cambridge, MA: Belknap Press/Harvard University Press, 2007).

seekers" authorized to make their own decisions regarding which religious texts, teachings, and practices have value and which do not.[3] Lyon has put his finger on a central challenge for a contemporary Catholic leadership that has struggled mightily with its loss of the coercive power to enforce right practice and right belief.

Vincent Miller has brilliantly analyzed the powerful cultural forces in a consumer society that can render religious beliefs, symbols, and practices into free-floating religious items that are wrenched from the thick communal frameworks that traditionally gave them meaning. The result is a form of commodified religion.[4] According to Miller, many Catholics today engage the Catholic faith according to the "interpretive habits" of the consumer. Staf Hellemans sees the same development but in a more positive light; he posits the rise of a new Catholic form, "choice Catholicism."[5] To these cultural factors we must add the failings of the Catholic Church itself: the scandal of clerical sexual abuse and the subsequent episcopal cover-up, tepid preaching, poor catechesis, a rigid dogmatism, and a general ministerial complacency regarding Catholic membership.

This is all by way of saying that Catholic Church leadership is right to be concerned about the postmodern fragility of religious identity. In response to this cultural and religious diagnosis, however, too many church leaders, particularly in the United States, have enacted a program of Catholic neotriumphalism and magisterial activism that is doomed to failure. We see this Catholic neotriumphalism in the determination to "walk back" many of the gains made in the postconciliar period in the areas of ecumenism and interreligious

---

[3] David Lyon, *Jesus in Disneyland: Religion in Postmodern Times* (Malden, MA: Blackwell, 2000), 34.

[4] Vincent J. Miller, *Consuming Religion: Christian Faith and Practice in a Consumer Culture* (New York: Continuum, 2004); Miller, "When Mediating Structures Change: The Magisterium, the Media, and the Culture Wars," in *When the Magisterium Intervenes: The Magisterium and Theologians in Today's Church*, ed. Richard R. Gaillardetz (Collegeville, MN: Liturgical Press, 2012), 154–74.

[5] Staf Hellemans, "Tracking the New Shape of the Catholic Church in the West," in *Towards a New Catholic Church in Advanced Modernity: Transformation, Visions, Tensions*, ed. Staf Hellemans and Jozef Wissink (Zürich: Lit Verlag, 2012), 19–50, at 24–37.

dialogue. In their place we find starkly contrastive assertions of a superior Catholic form of religious identity. Where Vatican II encouraged an ecumenical impulse that began with what we shared with other Christians, the neotriumphalism of today, a sturdy remnant of the hierocratic form, celebrates what distinguishes Catholicism from other Christian traditions in both liturgy and catechesis.[6] A mature Catholic identity, it is assumed, must be defined over against . . . what? Protestantism? A rapacious secularism? Political liberalism? The Democratic Party? This contrastive approach speaks to the fundamental problem with the Catholic importation of the culture wars—Catholic identity in a contrastive key is, in a basic sense, not very *catholic*.

Accompanying this neotriumphalist tendency has been an aggressive program of magisterial activism. Characterized by coercive ecclesiastical power (e.g., silencing or denouncing theologians, blacklisting doctrinally suspect speakers, chastising "disobedient" individuals and organizations, policing every forum devoted to ecclesial conversation), this activism presumes the surprisingly untraditional binary of orthodoxy and dissent. Within this binary framework, orthodoxy denotes a narrowly conceived articulation of the tradition that admits of no theological diversity, no constructive disagreement, no respectful criticism, and no open questions. Church doctrine achieves a troubling form within this framework. Juan Luis Segundo describes a "digital" conception of doctrine in which our doctrinal tradition is purged of its imaginative, transformative, and even mystagogical character and rendered strictly informational.[7] Not surprisingly, within the orthodoxy-dissent binary, dissent names everything that

---

[6] See the statement by the Vatican's Congregation for Divine Worship and the Discipline of the Sacraments regarding principles for liturgical translation, *Liturgiam Authenticam*, 40: "great caution is to be taken to avoid a wording or style that the Catholic faithful would confuse with the manner of speech of non-Catholic ecclesial communities or of other religions." Available online at http://www.vatican.va/roman_curia/congregations/ccdds/ documents/rc_con_ccdds _doc_20010507_liturgiam-authenticam_en.html. This principle is clearly in evidence in the recent English translation of the Roman Missal.

[7] Juan Luis Segundo, *The Liberation of Dogma: Faith, Revelation, and Dogmatic Teaching Authority*, trans. Philip Berryman (Maryknoll, NY: Orbis Books, 1992), 108.

stands outside this univocal, "orthodox" rendering of the tradition. Miller observes a shift during the pontificate of John Paul II away from doctrinal fidelity as a commitment to the central convictions of the Christian faith and toward doctrinal fidelity as a rigorous defense of the outer boundaries of religious identity.[8] In a similar vein, Nicholas Lash argues that one of the most pervasive failings of the church's teaching ministry is the modern Catholic tendency to reduce doctrinal teaching to mere governance.[9] When we conceive of the teaching ministry of the church as governance, we will naturally look to our teachers to "police" the faith and imagine the appropriate response to such teaching less as understanding and more as obedience.

A more constructive and potentially fruitful alternative would be to pursue a more compelling formation of Catholic identity, one sustained by the tethered ecclesial virtues of magnanimity and humility.

Forming a "Magnanimous" Catholic Identity

The cultivation of the ecclesial virtue of magnanimity, when tethered to the ecclesial virtue of humility, could encourage a robust and compelling account of the Catholic Christian faith that is rooted in the Gospel yet purged of any neotriumphalist leanings.[10] In some progressive Catholic circles, there is a reflex attitude of vague embarrassment when it comes to the Catholic Church today. Sensitive to the excesses of Catholic neotriumphalism, some Catholics have responded with a kind of ecclesial self-flagellation that is overeager to confess the failings of contemporary Catholicism at the expense of a positive account of what Catholic Christianity has to offer the

[8] Vincent J. Miller, "Ecclesiology, Cultural Change, and the Changing Nature of Culture," in *A Church with Open Doors: Catholic Ecclesiology for the Third Millennium*, ed. Richard R. Gaillardetz and Edward P. Hahnenberg (Collegeville, MN: Liturgical Press, 2015), 79.

[9] Nicholas Lash, "Authors, Authority, and Authorization," in *Authority in the Roman Catholic Church: Theory and Practice*, ed. Bernard Hoose (Burlington, VT: Ashgate Publishers, 2002), 65.

[10] Richard R. Gaillardetz, "Do We Need a New(-er) Apologetics?," *America* 190, no. 3 (February 2, 2004): 26–33.

world today. Theologians can get stuck in the critical task of delineating the distortions and systemic power inequities that exist in the church and its tradition and thereby overlook Catholicism's many gifts and insights.

We live in a world struggling under the burdens of massive economic inequities and the horrific global scourges on human dignity of human trafficking, regional violence, and even genocide. Anthony Carroll notes:

> The secular horizon of modern societies is often poorly equipped to deal with the tragic aspects of human life such as illness, suffering, and death. Short of resources of existential meaning, purely secular programs in advanced modernity often turn to chemical solutions to extinguish the pain and existential angst that face us at such times. These solutions, whilst having an important contribution to make, do not provide adequate support in these moments of human life.[11]

In response to such a world, the Catholic Church can offer a vital message grounded in the liberative Gospel of Jesus Christ. The richly Christocentric orientation of the council's teaching provides the foundation for an ecclesial magnanimity eager to offer the world the Good News of Jesus Christ. As we saw in chapter 6, it is this robust Christocentrism that Pope Francis is appropriating in his own pastoral program.

In a consumer culture saturated by the ubiquitous process of commodification and the inexorable embrace of an atomistic individualism, Catholicism can draw from an extraordinarily rich spiritual tradition and sacramental imagination capable of reinvigorating the meaning and value of daily human existence. Here in the United States, the tremendous popularity of spiritual writers like Kathleen Norris, Richard Rohr, Joan Chittister, Ron Rolheiser, Robert Barron, and James Martin speaks to the enduring relevance of this heritage.

Catholic teaching must not be reduced to a set of museum pieces with the church minister as its curator. Any effective presentation of Catholic teaching must speak to human experience. There must be a firm conviction that, as James Bacik puts it, "human experi-

---

[11] Anthony J. Carroll, "A Catholic Program for Advanced Modernity," in Hellemans and Wissink, 51–77, at 64.

ence and Christian doctrines are connected not simply logically and externally but organically and intrinsically."[12] If church teaching is true, as we believe it to be, it will illuminate daily living. This means that an effective presentation of the Catholic faith must be attuned to ordinary human experience if it is to make a difference in people's lives. When we teach of sin and the reconciling love of God made manifest in Christ, these cannot be left as abstractions. They are terms, doctrines, and concepts that will speak to people only to the extent that they help interpret the gently wafting melodies and jolting dissonances already playing in their life stories. We must be convinced that God's revelation gives meaning not only to the few precious hours of "religious time" we fight to preserve for going to church, reading the Bible, or for formal prayer but also to our most mundane human engagements.

Such a magnanimous Catholic identity must be culturally engaged. It would have to consider human culture as the place wherein humanity's glory and banality, sin and grace, despair and hope are all given expression. It must proceed from the confident conviction that in political events, the visual arts, music, fiction, theatre and film, family leisure, and family grieving, we encounter the drama of human salvation and, for those with eyes to see, intimations of the divine. Examples of this kind of cultural engagement abound. One sees it in Leo O'Donovan's many articles in *America* explicating the deep theological significance of great works of art. We see it in Robert Barron's masterful theological exploration of literature and film on his blog, *Word on Fire*. We see it across a broad ideological spectrum in the Catholic political engagements of public intellectuals like E. J. Dionne, John Gehring, Cathleen Kaveny, Maryann Cusinamo Love, George Weigel, Robert George, Mary Ann Glendon, and Helen Alvare.

To a younger generation yearning for causes worthy of their idealism, Catholicism supports avenues for vigorous social engagement commensurate with a body of social teaching that presents thoughtful and compelling approaches to the massive problems facing our world today—global climate change, the plight of refugees, human trafficking, and massive income inequity. Youth ministers and college

---

[12] James J. Bacik, *Apologetics and the Eclipse of Mystery: Mystagogy According to Karl Rahner* (Notre Dame, IN: University of Notre Dame Press, 1980), 13.

campus ministers give widespread testimony to the popularity and transformative potential of service immersion trips and yearlong service programs like the Jesuit Volunteer Corps and Rostro de Cristo that allow young adults to witness the transformative power of social Catholicism in action.

The excesses of contemporary Catholic neotriumphalism are best compensated not by obsessive reproach but by an eager rediscovery of the still liberating and inspirational power of contemporary Catholic faith.

Forming a "Humble" Catholic Identity

A renewed Catholic identity formed in a nontriumphalist key must, however, augment the virtue of magnanimity that celebrates the Catholic faith's many gifts and considerable pastoral promise with the ecclesial virtue of humility. Contemporary Catholicism's greatest scandal is the fear of scandal itself. The episcopal malfeasance that led bishops to cover up instances of sexual abuse was too often motivated by a misguided fear of scandal. The ecclesiastical preoccupation with the vigorous defense of the church's good reputation blinded too many leaders to the harm that was being done and ended up doing far greater damage to the very reputation they sought to protect.

Closely connected to this obsessive fear of scandal is the preoccupation with "confusing the faithful" that is often presented as the justification for a rigorous doctrinal policing of theologians, pastoral ministers, and public speakers. Many perceive church teaching from within an interpretive horizon famously described by Bernard Lonergan as "classical consciousness." Within this framework, historical change is largely accidental in character and divine truth is seen as unchanging, objective, and ahistorical. On matters of doctrine, "classicists" are preoccupied with consistency, clarity, and certitude, often at the expense of achieving genuine historical understanding.[13] Rather than guiding the community of faith in the quest for

---

[13] See Bernard Lonergan, "The Transition from a Classicist Worldview to Historical Mindedness" and "The Dehellenization of Dogma," in *A Second Col-*

genuine religious understanding and meaning, they see themselves as guardians and purveyors of timeless certitudes. We encounter in this doctrinal activism a fear of admitting that there is a gradation in the authority of church teaching that opens up some (nondogmatic) teachings to revision and even reversal, or that there may be a wider realm of theologically open questions.

The antidote, I suggest, lies in the cultivation of the "doctrinal humility" that we addressed in chapter 4. In his classic work on ecclesial reform, Yves Congar warned, in particular, of the danger of the magisterium failing to recognize when it had entered into the realm of contingent realities, citing, as but one example, the Galileo affair.[14] In a recent essay, Charles Taylor has decried the persistent failure to acknowledge the contingent elements embedded in certain church teaching.[15] He offers the example of Pope Paul VI's teaching on birth regulation and John Paul II's reframing of that teaching within his much-discussed "theology of the body." One could extend this concern further to recent magisterial teaching on the intrinsic evil of homosexual acts. Catholic theologians must be willing to press church leaders to consider whether they have taken sufficient account of our largely contingent and rapidly evolving understanding of human sexuality.[16]

The failure to embrace a necessary doctrinal humility is also evident when church leaders speak out in areas concerned with public policy. In spring 2010, the US Catholic bishops declared their opposition to the Obama administration's "Affordable Care Act," expressing concern that a set of complex legislative provisions did not provide sufficient protection against the federal funding of abortions. The

---

lection: Papers, ed. William F. J. Ryan and Bernard J. Tyrrell (Toronto: University of Toronto Press, 1996), 1–9, 11–12.

[14] Yves Congar, *Vrai et fausse réforme dans l'Église*, rev. ed. (Paris: Cerf, 1968), 164; translated into English as *True and False Reform in the Church*, trans. Paul Philibert (Collegeville, MN: Liturgical Press, 2011), 154.

[15] Charles Taylor, "Magisterial Authority," in *The Crisis of Authority in Catholic Modernity*, ed. Michael Lacey and Francis Oakley (New York: Oxford University Press, 2011), 259–69.

[16] Pope Francis's frequent denunciations of gender theory leave him vulnerable to the criticism that he has assumed too much regarding the providentially given structure of human sexuality.

bishops certainly had a right to present their position on the issue and Catholics were obligated to attend carefully to their position. The problem lay not with the bishops' judgment of the merits of this legislation but with their failure to properly modulate their judgment and acknowledge when they had left the realm of church doctrine and entered the realm of complex prudential judgments about which faithful Catholics could freely disagree.

If we are to cultivate a Catholic identity that is both magnanimous and humble, we must also resist the deeply polarizing ideological divides facing the Roman Catholic Church today. The current editor-in-chief of the Jesuit journal *America*, Matt Malone, published a manifesto of sorts in June 2013, outlining the direction he hoped that journal would take under his leadership. He expressed a quite legitimate fear regarding the ways in which the hyperpartisanship of the American political scene was colonizing the life of the church. "As a result, the terms and the tenor of the ecclesiastical conversation become increasingly indistinguishable from those of the larger culture. For our part, the Catholic media become the ecclesiastical equivalent of the cable news lineup: everybody has a favorite outlet, and more often than not it is the one that caters best to our preexisting views."[17] This led Malone to disavow the language of "liberal," "moderate," "conservative" as inappropriate importations of political categories into the life of the church. For Malone, the authentic communion proper to a community of disciples should preclude such ideological identifications.

I am sympathetic with much of what Fr. Malone has to say here. The ideological polarization evident among church elites (i.e., the clergy, pastoral ministers, theologians, church commentators) is all too evident. The solution, however, does not lie in the naïve renunciation of labels. There are real differences among us and these differences usually cohere around certain patterns and structures of Catholic identity. Traditionalists vs. progressives, *aggiornamento* vs. *ressourcement*, people of God vs. *communio*, pro-life vs. social justice—these dyads are problematic because they risk reducing the richness and, well, the

---

[17] Matt Malone, "Pursuing the Truth in Love," *America* 208, no. 19 (June 3–10, 2013). Available online at: http://americamagazine.org/issue/pursuing -truth-love.

catholicity of Catholic identity. At the same time, I suspect that some recourse to shorthand labels is unavoidable. In the life of the church, we often encounter Catholics with whom we are deeply simpatico and others whose appropriation of the faith seems to us foreign and even alienating. There are deep differences among us, and the solution cannot lie in disavowing labels as if the divisions they name would also disappear. The challenge is to take seriously the "otherness" of those with whom we disagree without demonizing them. The challenge is to cultivate the habits of "holy conversation" that lead us to learn from another. The solution may involve the *First Things* readership dipping more regularly into the pages of *Commonweal* and the readers of *National Catholic Reporter* spending a little time with the other NCR, the *National Catholic Register*.

What we need is the recovery of the catholicity of dialogue that we saw at work at the council. This commitment has a distinguished pedigree in our tradition. The very structure of St. Thomas Aquinas's magnificent *Summa* suggests something of the humility presupposed in the catholicity of dialogue. The *Summa* is structured in the form of a respectful, deeply textured conversation with those who held views different from his own. Thomas once cited with approval the position of Aristotle on how to deal with those with whom we disagree. In his commentary on the *Metaphysics of Aristotle*, Thomas wrote:

> In selecting and rejecting opinions a person should not be led by love or hate concerning who said them but by the certitude of truth. So he [Aristotle] says we should love both: those whose opinions we follow, and those whose opinions we reject. For both study to find the truth and in this way they are our collaborators.[18]

Here again we are drawn to the example of Pope Francis who exhorted those at the synod of the family not to fear lively debate and disagreement.

We live in a society subject to what Miller calls the "heterogenization of culture."[19] It is tempting for us to take refuge in our own ideological niches that function as a kind of echo chamber, reassuring

---

[18] Thomas Aquinas, *Commentary on the Metaphysics of Aristotle* (Turin: Marietti, 1950), Book 12, 9, 599.

[19] Miller, "When Mediating Structures Change," 160–62.

us of the obvious superiority of our own positions. One of the iro-
nies of the "Information Age" is that many were hopeful that these
new communications technologies would overcome this cultural
balkanization and facilitate meaningful public conversation with
those who differ from us in substantive ways. To date, that promise
has not been realized. *New York Times* columnist David Brooks has
noted how the internet and our more segmented society have too
often worked *against* the development of a more tolerant and open-
minded citizenry. Why? Brooks writes:

> Once you've joined a side, the information age makes it easier for you
> to surround yourself with people like yourself. . . . We don't only want
> radio programs and Web sites from members of our side—we want
> to live near people like ourselves. . . . So every place becomes more
> like itself, and the cultural divides between places become stark. The
> information age was supposed to make distance dead, but because of
> clustering, geography becomes more important. . . . Many of us find
> ourselves living in places that are overwhelmingly liberal or overwhelm-
> ingly conservative. When we find ourselves in such communities, our
> views shift even further in the dominant direction. You get this self-
> reinforcement cycle going, which social scientists call "group polariza-
> tion." People lose touch with others in opposing, now distant, camps.
> And millions of kids are raised in what amount to political ghettoes.[20]

The habits of holy conversation require us to seek out and engage
those with whom we are likely to disagree in the hope of discovering or
achieving some basis for mutual understanding and respect from which
we can more productively deal with areas of substantive disagreement.

Learning to Wrestle with the Catholic Tradition

There are elements of "choice Catholicism" that are quite positive. They speak to the maturation of adult Catholics capable of
distinguishing between those elements of Catholic faith and practice
that are central and supportive of a life of authentic discipleship
and those that are not. Still, it seems to me that Catholics must

---

[20] David Brooks, "Age of Political Segregation," *New York Times* (June 29, 2004).

also resist elements of choice Catholicism that play into a hyperindividualistic and consumerist ethos. Postmodern religion has been profoundly influenced by our culture of choice. Within that culture, we are tempted to see our tradition as a religious grab bag in which we are free to pull out whatever we find appealing. As we noted earlier, for many church leaders the default reaction to this situation is to return to the juridical paradigm of "command and obey" and insist on an uncritical and unswerving obedience to all church teaching. What we get are fidelity oaths imposed on ministers and church employees. Too many bishops are inclined to micromanage curricular and textbook decisions in Catholic schools and parish religious education programs. This kind of rigid dogmatism is both wrongheaded and futile as a form of resistance.

But there is another way beyond the inadequacies of "cafeteria," "consumer," or "choice" Catholicism; it is to encourage a form of active Catholic engagement constituted by a substantive and deliberate "wrestling with the tradition." To belong to a religious tradition requires that I take that tradition seriously, even, and perhaps especially, when it troubles me, and even when, at the end of the day, I find that I cannot give an unqualified adherence to it.

Consider two Catholic converts, Michael and Marie, who soon after having been received into the church have discovered the Catholic Church's teaching that the use of *in vitro* fertilization to assist in having a child is always morally wrong. Learning of this, Michael rejects the teaching immediately as silly and unworthy of his consideration. For him it is another example of the Catholic obsession with sex that made him pause before becoming Catholic in the first place. He never gives the teaching another thought. Marie, however, wrestles with the teaching, researching the scientific and medical dimensions of the issue while trying to grasp the moral arguments behind the church's teaching. She actually reads a recent Vatican statement on the topic and finds herself in sympathy with the official teaching's concern about the dangers of the technological commodification of human reproduction and the risk of eugenics. She spends considerable time in prayer and reflection on the matter and finds that, although she has come to appreciate the considerable insight in the Catholic Church's official position, she can still imagine instances in which *in vitro* fertilization might be warranted.

We might conclude that Marie ends up at the same place as Michael since neither can give a full and unqualified assent to this teaching. In fact, many of the "orthodoxy police" would dismiss both as "dissenters," but is their status really the same? I would argue that it is not. Michael was in no way troubled by this particular teaching; he simply ignored it. His cavalier attitude suggests a general unwillingness to deeply engage the controversial elements of the Catholic tradition. His Catholic identity is likely to remain relatively superficial. Marie, in contrast, may not have found that she could fully embrace the teaching, but she came to appreciate some of the ethical arguments of the official Catholic position in a way she hadn't earlier. She now has a much greater sensitivity to some of the dangers associated with an unfettered use of reproductive technologies. Her wrestling with the teaching, although it did not end in an internal assent, has impacted her in significant ways. She has been shaped by her tradition and, perhaps just as important, she has decided to remain a part of a larger ecclesial conversation that may allow her difficulties and insights to shape that tradition, even if only by some modest increment. The integrity of Marie's struggles offers a model of what an authentically magnanimous yet humble Catholic identity might look like.

Pope Francis's Ecclesial Examination of Conscience

Pope Francis has offered the world a remarkable example of how the ecclesial virtue of humility can reinvigorate the Catholic faith. Whether it is his washing the feet of residents in a juvenile prison or his refusal to reside in the papal apartment, this Latin American pope exudes a spirituality exhibiting the transformative, joyful power of authentic humility.

We saw in chapter 4 that the heart of ecclesial humility lies in honest self-assessment. A humble church can never forget its true reality as the body of Christ and the temple of the Holy Spirit. At the same time a humble church must never forget that it is always also God's pilgrim people ever in need of reform and renewal. This harsh truth is more often observed in the breach by church leaders, or couched in pious banalities. Pope Francis will have none of that and has made honest ecclesial self-assessment the cornerstone of his pontificate. In December 2014, he addressed the Roman Curia and offered a bracing example of this kind of ecclesial self-assessment.[21] His frank admission of frustration with the attitudes of many of his closest advisers called to mind the frankness of Pope John's opening address at the council in which he admonished many of his closest advisers for being prophets of gloom. Francis was speaking to the members of the Roman Curia, to be sure, and much of what he addressed concerned maladies he believed had become rampant in the Vatican bureaucracy. The curial illnesses he diagnosed, however, represent dangers present to all who hold positions of leadership in the church and, to a certain extent, to all baptized Christians.

The pope began this remarkable address with the suggestion that church leaders too often act as if they were "lords of the manor," forgetting the spirit of humility and generosity that ought to characterize their ministry. He then listed a series of ecclesial "illnesses" that we need to be wary of: (1) the danger of being "immortal, immune, or indispensable," and avoiding the need for healthy self-criticism; (2) the disease of "industriousness," losing oneself in one's work and failing to attend to the need for rest, leisure, and renewal; (3) the illness of "mental and spiritual hardening" in which one's work hardens one to the simple joys and griefs of ordinary people; (4) a "functionalism" that so relies on planning and control and the preservation of the status quo that there is left little room for the work of the Spirit in acts of spontaneity and creativity; (5) the ecclesial malady of "poor communication" in which people become comfortable with working within their own self-contained siloes, losing track of the contributions of people in other areas, departments, or churches; (6) a "spiritual Alzheimer's disease" that is a forgetfulness of how dependent we are on God's saving work and the love of God that should animate our lives; (7) the disease of "rivalry" that leads to a preoccupation with honors, titles, and ecclesiastical status; (8) an "existential schizophrenia" that allows us to lead "double lives" such that our Christian service becomes bureaucratized and separated from the real concerns of the people we are to serve; (9) the

---

[21] A summary of the address can be accessed online at http://www.news.va/en /news/pope-francis-christmas-greetings-to-curia.

disease of "gossip" in which we easily content ourselves with sharing petty judgments of others in ways that inevitably sow the seeds of "discord"; (10) the danger of "deifying leaders" that happens when we become opportunists and careerists concerned with getting ahead rather than doing our work with integrity; (11) the disease of "indifference," a failure to attend to the needs and concerns of others or to encourage others, often out of jealousy; (12) the disease of a "funereal face" in which a melancholic spirit leads to rigidity and severity in place of the joy of the Gospel that should animate all believers; (13) the disease of "accumulation" in which we hide from our spiritual emptiness through the endless pursuit of material satisfactions; (14) the illness of "closed circles" that occurs when church members allow a tight group identification to prevent one from reaching out beyond their inner circle to other members of the church; (15) the disease of "worldly profit and exhibitionism" that transforms authentic Christian service into dominating power.

Francis has rehabilitated the virtue of humility from its many pious counterfeits. He possesses a magnanimous confidence in the evangelical power of the Good News of Jesus Christ. This power is liberating, however, only to the extent that it is exercised with the humility of a missionary disciple committed to ongoing conversion and confident that, in attending to the "other" as a person of infinite value, one finds the deepest meaning and purpose of one's own life.

The Christian "Disciplining of Power"

Recall that the final spiritual disease that Pope Francis listed was the temptation to turn authentic Christian service into dominating power. Any substantive pastoral reform in the spirit of the council will need to address the rampant spread of this spiritual illness. In chapter 5, I proposed a noncompetitive account of the church that calls for the redemption of ecclesial power and the appropriation of a new set of ecclesial habits regarding the exercise of power. Christians are recipients of God's saving action and agents of God's reconciling power. St. Paul reminds us that God "who reconciled us to himself through Christ . . . has given us the ministry of reconciliation" (1 Cor 5:18). The work of reconciliation accomplished in Jesus of Nazareth, through the power of the Spirit, is to continue in the mission of the church. In service of this mission, the church must become a school of discipleship in which dominating power and a preoccupation with control are transformed into the power of reconciliation and service. In that school we acquire habits of power appropriate to followers of Jesus.

How might we conceptualize the kind of ecclesial reform that could bring about this redemption of power? A surprising resource lies in the work of the French poststructuralist Michel Foucault. Foucault's enormous body of work challenged the zero-sum conception of power that we discussed in chapter 5. For Foucault, power is not a discrete and quantifiable entity or force but a reality that inheres within all relational networks. Power in this sense is ubiquitous, moving in all directions. There is never really a question of the presence or absence of power, only how it is "disciplined" within particular "technologies" or mechanisms of power. Foucault offered a now-classic analysis of the history of the Western penal system as but one example of a "technology" of power governed by the logic of domination and control. He persuasively demonstrated that the penal system disciplined power in ways that affected both prisoners and guards alike.[22]

There is much that a program for ecclesial reform and renewal can glean from Foucault's analysis. Just as Foucault complained that contemporary accounts of power are too preoccupied with the sovereign power of the state, so too in the life of the church, our analysis of power has been overly dependent on conceptions of juridical power regulated by canon law. Catholic theology, without ignoring the role of juridical power, must recover that more comprehensive dimension of ecclesial power that comes from baptism and is animated by the Spirit.

Foucault's conviction that networks of power are often concerned with domination and control certainly finds confirmation in the harmful structures and habits of power enacted in the Catholic Church, past and present. The invisibility of these networks of control and domination, often obscured by high-minded spiritual rhetoric,

---

[22] Michel Foucault, *Discipline and Punish: The Birth of the Prison* (New York: Vintage, 1977).

makes these mechanisms all the more dangerous. This is evident in the tragic and grievous abuse of children perpetrated under the veil of ecclesiastical respectability.

Particularly helpful is Foucault's conviction that power is not exercised unidirectionally. Those "in power" are affected as much by its exercise as are those who are the supposed objects of that power. As James Davison Hunter puts it, "Power always generates its own resistances. . . . Even the weak possess the power to challenge, subvert, destabilize and oppose. It may not be easy and it may even be costly, but the power to act is always present within the relations of power itself."[23] This analysis reminds us that church reform cannot settle with a simple redistribution of power (e.g., giving more power to pastoral councils); it must seek a fundamental transformation of the very way that power is conceived and exercised.

If a program for reform and renewal is to effect real and lasting change in church life, it must work toward the systemic redemption of power. Power can be subverted, transformed, and redirected in alternative and unanticipated ways. From the perspective of Christian discipleship, we can imagine communal exercises for the "disciplining" of power, that is, certain Christian "technologies of power" that may be entirely appropriate to the church's mission.[24] As a school of noncompetitive Christian discipleship, the church must establish and sustain distinctive "technologies of power" that transform power from the habits of domination to habits of power exercised in accord with the values of God's reign.

We already have instances in which this redemption of power is in evidence. The Eucharist, when it is ritually enacted in ways that fully display its transformative potential (that is, not simply as a display of clerical power and prerogative), offers such an alternative disciplining, as do family practices of forgiveness, hospitality, and generosity that

[23] James Davison Hunter, *To Change the World: The Irony, Tragedy, and Possibility of Christianity in the Late Modern World* (New York: Oxford University Press, 2010), 179.

[24] James K. A. Smith, *Who's Afraid of Postmodernism? Taking Derrida, Lyotard, and Foucault to Church*, The Church and Postmodern Culture Series (Grand Rapids, MI: Baker Academic, 2006), 102.

constitute the household as a "domestic church."[25] Parishes discipline the exercise of power in their outreach to the poor, their ministries of reconciliation—sacramental and nonsacramental—and in their practices of solidarity with the marginalized. Christian activists offer an alternative exercise of power when they put the vulnerability of their own bodies into play through nonviolent protest at police stations, abortion clinics, military bases, and border crossings.

The Rule of Benedict, one of the most authoritative sources for guidance in Western monasticism, represents a classic manual for the Christian disciplining of power.[26] The life of the monastery is to be disciplined through the integration of prayer and labor. It is to be so structured as to accommodate hospitality to the stranger. The exercise of power by the abbot is similarly disciplined. Chapter 3 of the Rule attends to the obligation of the abbot to consult the monks before making any decision of note, including the youngest members of the monastery. Within weeks of his papal election, Pope Francis provided a dramatic example of an alternative disciplining of ecclesial power when he celebrated an ancient Holy Thursday ritual not by washing the feet of twelve males, as liturgical law dictated, but by attending a juvenile prison and washing the feet of troubled youth, including women and Muslims.

Fifty years after the council, we are still waiting for a comprehensive program of church reform dedicated to the appropriate and necessary transformation of ecclesiastical structures. The focus of such a program would be to develop alternative ways to discipline ecclesial power in keeping with the Gospel. Such institutional reform is not a "liberal" project bent on accommodation to the values of the secular world, as is so often suggested; it is the necessary reform of a church that wishes to be more deeply rooted in the radical values

[25] Richard R. Gaillardetz, "The Christian Household as School of Discipleship: Reflections on the Ecclesial Contributions of the Christian Household to the Larger Church," in *The Household of God and Local Households: Revisiting the Domestic Church*, Bibliotheca Ephemeridum Theologicarum Lovaniensium Series, ed. Thomas Knieps-Port Le Roi, Gerard Mannion, and Peter De Mey (Leuven: Peeters, 2013), 111–21.

[26] Terrence G. Kardong, *Benedict's Rule: A Translation and Commentary* (Collegeville, MN: Liturgical Press, 1996).

of the Christian Gospel. It is a reform committed to unleashing the bountiful gifts of the Spirit lying dormant in our church.

For many in the church today, the abuse of power is associated with its ministerial structures. Whether the issue is sexual abuse or the exclusion of women from ministry, for many Catholics, ministerial structures and policies are experienced less as an instrument of reconciliation and healing than as vehicles for oppression and control. The most egregious instances of the systemic abuse of power, as with clerical sexual abuse, are easy to identify. More difficult to recognize are those customs and structures that have become so familiar that we have become blind to the extent of their dysfunction.

Consider the church's process of calling forth and forming candidates for ordination to the diocesan priesthood. I belong to a generation in which to come into adulthood as a single male who was also a practicing Catholic was to be peppered with questions about the possibility of a priestly vocation. These questions simply presupposed a particular theology of priestly vocation and a set of church structures (e.g., the office of the vocation director, seminaries) that supported that theology.[27] This theology of vocation presumed that a vocational calling was primarily a personal, interior reality, and that once it was juridically validated and ecclesiastically cultivated, the recipient would be granted ministerial power by way of sacramental ordination.

Our current structures and policies certainly support this assumption. When an individual presents himself to a diocesan vocation director with the claim that he might have a vocation to the priesthood, there will usually follow an initial investigation into whether there are canonical impediments to his ordination. There will also be, one hopes, some assessment of the candidate's sanctity and basic mental health. If no obstacles present themselves, the candidate will likely be accepted into the seminary. Now let us presume that over the course of his period of seminary formation, he passes all of his courses, dutifully attends daily Mass, sees his spiritual director regularly, and does not manifest heretical or "dangerous" views in his

---

[27] Edward Hahnenberg offers an informative consideration of the history of theologies of vocation in *Awakening Vocation: A Theology of Christian Call* (Collegeville, MN: Liturgical Press, 2010).

academic work, preaching, pastoral counseling, or field education. Even if this candidate manifests no aptitude for genuine pastoral leadership, is there any doubt he will be ordained? This vocational system is constructed more to discern impediments to ordination than to discern the existence of a charism or aptitude for the exercise of genuine pastoral leadership or pastoral ministry of any kind.

How might a program for church reform committed to redisciplining ecclesial power in keeping with the Gospel reimagine this vocational system? It would need to expand the pool of candidates in order to consider any and all who may be called by the Spirit to pastoral leadership. It would need to move away from an exclusive emphasis on personal sanctity, rigorous doctrinal orthodoxy, and the identification of impediments. Instead, it would cultivate ecclesial structures that allow the church to identify among its members those who possess the requisite charism for pastoral leadership. Such a charism would surely involve an aptitude for recognizing, empowering, and celebrating the gifts of others.

In this concluding chapter I have explored two avenues for church reform and renewal suggested by the council's encouragement of ecclesial humility and a noncompetitive account of ecclesial dynamics. These reflections suggest, I hope, something of how a more synthetic reading of the council might inform a pastoral program for reform and renewal today. Any such program of renewal will have to reckon with the reality that twenty or fifty or a hundred years from now, a new council may have to undertake a new building project, one that would react to the inevitable inadequacies of Vatican II's ecclesial vision for the church of 2035, 2065, or 2115. That council would face a similar task, drawing creatively from our great tradition even as it engaged in a discerning reading of the signs of those future times.

What might such a council have on its agenda? Surely it would have to respond to the lacunae of Vatican II. It would have to provide a more adequate and comprehensive account of ministry that better attended to the new ministerial forms that have emerged and flourished since Vatican II. It might seek out a more compelling theological anthropology capable of responding effectively to pressing questions of sex and gender. It almost certainly will draw more fully from the theological and cultural resources of the churches of the global South. Sadly, it may also have to address the calamitous consequences of global climate change. We cannot fully anticipate the agenda of some future council. We can commit ourselves to a pastoral program of reform and renewal inspired by a thoroughly pastoral council. And, in the end, all that we can ask of our church today, or in any age, is that it be faithful to its most precious gift, the Good News of Jesus Christ, and courageous in its engagement with the world, confident that the Spirit will guide us into the mysterious future of God's reign.

Bibliography

Alberigo, Giuseppe, and Joseph A. Komonchak, eds. *History of Vatican II*. 5 vols. Maryknoll, NY: Orbis Books, 1995–2006.

Allen, John L., Jr. *Against the Tide: The Radical Leadership of Pope Francis*. Liguori, MO: Liguori Publications, 2014.

Austin, Gerard. "Restoring Equilibrium after the Struggle with Heresy." In *Source and Summit: Commemorating Josef A. Jungmann, S.J.*, edited by Joanne M. Pierce and Michael Downey, 35–47. Collegeville, MN: Liturgical Press, 1999.

Beal, John. "It Shall Not Be So Among You: Crisis in the Church: Crisis in Church Law." In *Governance, Accountability and the Future of the Catholic Church*, edited by Francis Oakley and Bruce Russett, 88–102. New York: Continuum, 2004.

Bellarmine, Robert. *De Conciliis, et Ecclesia, De Controversiis: Christianae Fidei Adversus Haereticos*. Rome: Giunchi et Menicanti, 1836.

Bevans, Stephan B., and Roger P. Schroeder. *Constants in Context: A Theology of Mission for Today*. Maryknoll, NY: Orbis Books, 2004.

Bevans, Stephen B. "Revisiting Mission at Vatican II: Theology and Practice for Today's Missionary Church." *Theological Studies* 74 (June 2013): 261–83.

Boulding, Mary Cecily. "The Doctrine of the Holy Spirit in the Documents of Vatican II." *Irish Theological Quarterly* 51 (1985): 253–67.

Charue, André-Marie. "Le Saint-Esprit dans 'Lumen Gentium.'" *Ephemerides theologicae lovanienses* 45 (1969): 358–79.

Clifford, Catherine. "L'herméneutique d'un principe herméneutique: La hiérarchie des verites." In *L'Autorité et les autorités: L'herméneutique théo- logique de Vatican II*, edited by Gilles Routhier and Guy Jobin, 69–91. Paris: Cerf, 2010.

———. *Decoding Vatican II: Interpretation and Ongoing Reception*. New York: Paulist Press, 2014.

Congar, Yves, and Guilherme Baraúna, eds. *L'Église de Vatican II*. 3 vols. [*Unam Sanctam* 51 a-c]. Paris: Cerf, 1967.

Congar, Yves. *I Believe in the Holy Spirit*. 3 vols. New York: Seabury, 1983.

———. *L'Église de Saint Augustin à l'époque moderne*. Paris: Cerf, 1970.

———. *Lay People in the Church*. Rev. ed. London: Geoffrey Chapman, 1985.

———. *My Journal of the Council*. Collegeville, MN: Liturgical Press, 2012.

———. "Titres donnés au pape." In *Concilium* 108 (1975): 55–64.

———. *True and False Reform in the Church*. Collegeville, MN: Liturgical Press, 2011.

Cornille, Catherine. *The Im-possibility of Interreligious Dialogue*. New York: Crossroad, 2008.

Crowley, Paul, ed. *From Vatican II to Pope Francis: Charting a Catholic Future*. Maryknoll, NY: Orbis, 2014.

D'Antonio, William V., Michelle Dillon, and Mary L. Gauthier. *American Catholics in Transition*. Lanham, MD: Rowman and Littlefield, 2013.

De Lubac, Henri. *Corpus Mysticum: The Eucharist and the Church in the Middle Ages; Historical Survey*. Notre Dame, IN: University of Notre Dame Press, 2006.

De Mey, Peter. "Church Renewal and Reform in the Documents of Vatican II: History, Theology, Terminology." *The Jurist* 71 (2011): 369–400.

Dolan, Jay P. *In Search of an American Catholicism*. New York: Oxford University Press, 2002.

Doyle, Dennis. *The Church Emerging from Vatican II : A Popular Approach to Contemporary Catholicism*. Mystic, CT: Twenty-Third Publications, 2002.

Duffy, Eamon. *The Stripping of the Altars: Traditional Religion in England c. 1400–c. 1580*. New Haven, CT: Yale University Press, 2005.

Dulles, Avery. *Models of Revelation*. Garden City, NY: Doubleday, 1983.

Euart, Sharon. "Structures for Participation in the Church." *Origins* 35 (May 26, 2005): 18–25.

Faggioli, Massimo. *Vatican II: The Battle for Meaning*. New York: Paulist Press, 2012.

———. *John XXIII: The Medicine of Mercy*. Collegeville, MN: Liturgical Press, 2014.

———. *True Reform: Liturgy and Ecclesiology in* Sacrosanctum Concilium. Collegeville, MN: Liturgical Press, 2012.

Faivre, Alesandre. *The Emergence of the Laity in the Early Church*. New York: Paulist Press, 1990.

Ferrone, Rita. *Liturgy:* Sacrosanctum Concilium. Rediscovering Vatican II Series. New York: Paulist Press, 2007.

Foucault, Michel. *Discipline and Punish: The Birth of the Prison*. New York: Vintage, 1977.

Francis, Pope. "A Big Heart Open to God: The Exclusive Interview with Pope Francis." By Antonio Spadaro. Translated by Massimo Faggioli, Sarah Christopher Faggioli, Dominic Robinson, Patrick Howell, and Griffin Oleynick. *America* 209, no. 8 (September 30, 2013): http://americamagazine.org/pope-interview.

———. *The Church of Mercy: A Vision for the Church.* Chicago: Loyola Press, 2014.

Fullam, Lisa. *The Virtue of Humility: A Thomistic Apologetic.* Lewiston, NY: Edwin Mellen Press, 2009.

Gaillardetz, Richard R. "Do We Need a New(er) Apologetics?" *America* 190, no. 3 (February 2, 2004): 26–33.

———. "The Christian Household as School of Discipleship: Reflections on the Ecclesial Contributions of the Christian Household to the Larger Church." In *The Household of God and Local Households: Revisiting the Domestic Church*, edited by Thomas Knieps-Port Le Roi, Gerard Mannion, and Peter De Mey, 111–21. Bibliotheca Ephemeridum Theologicarum Lovaniensium Series. Leuven: Peeters, 2013.

———. "The Ecclesiological Foundations of Ministry within an Ordered Communion." In *Ordering of the Baptismal Priesthood*, edited by Susan Wood, 26–51. Collegeville, MN: Liturgical Press, 2003.

———. *Teaching with Authority: A Theology of the Magisterium in the Church.* Collegeville, MN: Liturgical Press, 1997.

———. *The Church in the Making:* Lumen Gentium, Christus Dominus, Orientalium Ecclesiarum. Rediscovering Vatican II Series. New York: Paulist Press, 2006.

Garrigou-Lagrange, Reginald. *De Revelatione per Ecclesiam catholicam proposita.* 4th ed. Rome: Ferrari, 1945.

Gibaut, John St. H. *The* Cursus Honorum: *A Study of Origins and Evolution of Sequential Ordination.* Patristic Studies, vol. 3. Bern: Peter Lang, 2000.

Groome, Thomas H., and Michael J. Daley, eds. *Reclaiming Catholicism: Treasures Old and New.* Maryknoll, NY: Orbis Books, 2010.

Hahnenberg, Edward P. *Awakening Vocation: A Theology of Christian Call.* Collegeville, MN: Liturgical Press, 2010.

Haught, John. *The Revelation of God in History.* Wilmington, DE: Michael Glazier, 1988.

Hebblethwaite, Peter. *Pope Paul VI.* New York: Paulist Press, 1993.

Heft, James L., and John O'Malley, eds. *After Vatican II: Trajectories and Hermeneutics.* Grand Rapids, MI: Eerdmans, 2012.

Hellemans, Staf, and Jozef Wissink, eds. *Towards a New Catholic Church in Advanced Modernity: Transformation, Visions, Tensions.* Zürich: Lit Verlag, 2012.

Henn, William. *The Honor of My Brothers: A Brief History of the Relationship between the Pope and the Bishops*. New York: Crossroad, 2000.

Hinsdale, Mary Ann. "A Feminist Reflection on Postconciliar Catholic Ecclesiology." In *A Church with Open Doors: Catholic Ecclesiology for the Third Millennium*, edited by Richard R. Gaillardetz and Edward P. Hahnenberg, 112–37. Collegeville, MN: Liturgical Press, 2015.

Hughson, Thomas. "Interpreting Vatican II: A New Pentecost," *Theological Studies* 69 (2008): 3–37.

Hunter, James Davison. *To Change the World: The Irony, Tragedy, and Possibility of Christianity in the Late Modern World*. New York: Oxford University Press, 2010.

Hurley, Denis. *Vatican II: Keeping the Dream Alive*. Pietermaritzburg, South Africa: Cluster Publications, 2005.

Ivereigh, Austen. *The Great Reformer: Francis and the Making of a Radical Pope*. New York: Henry Holt and Co., 2014.

Jounel, Pierre. "From the Council of Trent to Vatican Council II." In *The Church at Prayer*, vol. 1: *Principles of the Liturgy*, edited by. A. G. Mortimort, 63–84. Collegeville, MN: Liturgical Press, 1992.

Kardong, Terrence G. *Benedict's Rule: A Translation and Commentary*. Collegeville, MN: Liturgical Press, 1996.

Kasper, Walter. *The Catholic Church: Nature, Reality, and Mission*. New York: Bloomsbury, 2015.

Keenan, James F. *Moral Wisdom: Lessons and Texts from the Catholic Tradition*. Lanham, MD: Sheed and Ward, 2010.

Komonchak, Joseph. "Subsidiarity in the Church: The State of the Question." *The Jurist* 48 (1988): 298–349.

———. "The Significance of Vatican II for Ecclesiology." In *The Gift of the Church: A Textbook on Ecclesiology*, edited by Peter Phan, 69–92. Collegeville, MN: Liturgical Press, A Michael Glazier Book, 2000.

Küng, Hans. *The Council, Reform and Reunion*. New York: Sheed & Ward, 1961.

Lafont, Ghislain. *Imagining the Catholic Church: Structured Communion in the Spirit*. Collegeville, MN: Liturgical Press, 2000.

Lakeland, Paul. "'I Want to Be in That Number': Desire, Inclusivity and the Church." *CTSA Proceedings* 66 (2011): 16–28.

Lamb, Matthew L., and Matthew Levering, eds. *Vatican II: Renewal within Tradition*. New York: Oxford University Press, 2008.

Lash, Nicholas. "Authors, Authority, and Authorization." In *Authority in the Roman Catholic Church: Theory and Practice*, edited by Bernard Hoose, 59–71. Burlington, VT: Ashgate Publishers, 2002.

Levy, Ian Christopher. *Holy Scripture and the Quest for Authority at the End of the Middle Ages*. Notre Dame, IN: University of Notre Dame Press, 2012.

Leys, Ad. *Ecclesiological Impacts of the Principle of Subsidiarity*. Kampen: Kok, 1995.

Lyon, David. *Jesus in Disneyland: Religion in Postmodern Times*. Malden, MA: Blackwell, 2000.

Magnani, Giovanni. "Does the So-Called Theology of the Laity Possess a Theological Status?" In *Vatican II: Assessment and Perspectives*, edited by René Latourelle, 1:568–633. New York: Paulist Press, 1988.

Mannion, Gerard. *Ecclesiology and Postmodernity: Questions for the Church in Our Time*. Collegeville, MN: Liturgical Press, 2007.

Marini, Piero. *A Challenging Reform: Realizing the Vision of the Liturgical Renewal*. Collegeville, MN: Liturgical Press, 2007.

Markus, Robert A. *Christianity and the Secular*. Notre Dame, IN: University of Notre Dame Press, 2006.

Marmion, Columba. *Christ: The Ideal of the Priest*. St. Louis: Herder, 1952.

McEnroy, Carmel. *Guests in Their Own House: The Women of Vatican II*. New York: Crossroad, 1996. Reprint, Eugene, OR: Wipf and Stock, 2011.

Meeks, Wayne A. *The Origins of Christian Morality: The First Two Centuries*. New Haven, CT: Yale University Press, 1993.

Merton, Thomas. *The Wisdom of the Desert*. New York: New Directions, 1960.

Michalski, Melvin. *The Relationship between the Universal Priesthood of the Baptized and the Ministerial Priesthood of the Ordained in Vatican II and in Subsequent Theology*. Lewiston, NY: Mellen University Press, 1996.

Miller, Vincent J. "Ecclesiology, Cultural Change, and the Changing Nature of Culture." In *A Church with Open Doors: Catholic Ecclesiology for the Third Millennium*, edited by Richard R. Gaillardetz and Edward Hahnenberg, 64–84. Collegeville, MN: Liturgical Press, 2015.

———. "When Mediating Structures Change: The Magisterium, the Media, and the Culture Wars." In *When the Magisterium Intervenes: The Magisterium and Theologians in Today's Church*, edited by Richard R. Gaillardetz, 154–74. Collegeville, MN: Liturgical Press, 2012.

———. *Consuming Religion: Christian Faith and Practice in a Consumer Culture*. New York: Continuum, 2004.

Nichols, Terence L. *That All May Be One: Hierarchy and Participation in the Church*. Collegeville, MN: Liturgical Press, 1997.

Noonan, John. *The Church That Can and Cannot Change*. Notre Dame, IN: University of Notre Dame Press, 2005.

———. *The Scholastic Analysis of Usury*. Cambridge, MA: Harvard University Press, 1957.

O'Brien, John. "Ecclesiology as Narrative," *Ecclesiology* 4, no. 2 (2008): 148–65.

O'Callaghan, Joseph F. *Electing Our Bishops: How the Catholic Church Should Choose Its Leaders*. New York: Sheed and Ward, 2007.

O'Collins, Gerald. *Living Vatican II*. New York: Paulist Press, 2006.

———. *Rethinking Fundamental Theology: Toward a New Fundamental Theology*. Oxford: Oxford University Press, 2011.

O'Malley, John W. "Vatican II: Did Anything Happen?" *Theological Studies* 67 (2006): 3–33.

———. *What Happened at Vatican II*. Cambridge, MA: Harvard University Press, 2008.

Osborne, Kenan B. *Ministry: Lay Ministry in the Roman Catholic Church*. New York: Paulist Press, 1993.

Pesch, Christian. *Praelectiones dogmaticae*. 5th ed. Freiburg: Herder, 1915.

Philips, Gérard. *L'Église et son mystére au IIe Concile du Vatican*. 2 vols. Paris: Desclée, 1967.

Pottmeyer, Hermann J. *Towards a Papacy in Communion: Perspectives from Vatican Councils I & II*. New York: Crossroad, 1998.

Puglisi, James F. "Presider as *Alter Christus*, Head of the Body?" *Liturgical Ministry* 10 (Summer 2001): 153–58.

———. *The Process of Admission to Ordained Ministry*. Vol. 1: *Epistemological Principles and Roman Catholic Rites*. Collegeville, MN: Liturgical Press, 1996.

Ratzinger, Joseph. *Theological Highlights of Vatican II*. New York: Paulist Press, 1966.

Richard, Lucien, Daniel Harrington, and John W. O'Malley, eds. *Vatican II: The Unfinished Agenda*. New York: Paulist Press, 1987.

Routhier, Gilles. *Vatican II: Herméneutic et réception*. Quebec: Éditions Fides, 2006.

———. "Les réactions du cardinal Léger à la préparation de Vatican II." *Revue d'Histoire de l'Eglise de France* 80 (1994): 281–302.

———. "Vatican II: Relevance and Future." *Theological Studies* 74 (September 2013): 537–54.

Rush, Ormond. "The Australian Bishops of Vatican II: Participation and Reception." In *Vatican II: The Reception and Implementation in the Australian Church*, edited by Neil Ormerod, Ormond Rush, et al., 4–19. Melbourne: John Garrett, 2012.

———. *Still Interpreting Vatican II: Some Hermeneutical Principles*. New York: Paulist Press, 2004.

———. *The Eyes of Faith: The Sense of the Faithful and the Church's Reception of Revelation*. Washington, DC: The Catholic University of America Press, 2009.

Rynne, Xavier. *Vatican Council II*. New York: Farrar, Straus & Giroux, 1968.

Scharer, Matthias, and Bernd Jochen Hilberath. *The Practice of Communicative Theology*. New York: Crossroad, 2008.

Schatz, Klaus. *Papal Primacy: From Its Origins to the Present*. Collegeville, MN: Liturgical Press, 1996.

Schillebeeckx, Edward. "The Typological Definition of the Christian Layman according to Vatican II." In *The Mission of the Church*, 90–116. New York: Seabury Press, 1973.

———. *The Church with a Human Face*. New York: Crossroad, 1985.

———. *The Council Notes of Edward Schillebeeckx 1962–1963*, edited by Karim Schelkens. Leuven: Peeters, 2011.

Schüssler Fiorenza, Elisabeth. *Bread Not Stone: The Challenge of Feminist Hermeneutics*. Boston: Beacon Press, 1995.

———. *Discipleship of Equals: A Critical Feminist Ekklesialogy of Liberation*. New York: Crossroad, 1993.

Smith, Christian, Kyle Longest, Jonathan Hill, and Kari Christoffersen. *Young Catholic America: Emerging Adults In, Out of, and Gone from the Church*. New York: Oxford University Press, 2014.

Smith, James K. A. *Who's Afraid of Postmodernism? Taking Derrida, Lyotard, and Foucault to Church*. The Church and Postmodern Culture Series. Grand Rapids, MI: Baker Academic, 2006.

Suenens, Léo-Joseph. "A Plan for the Whole Council." In *Vatican II by Those Who Were There*, edited by Alberic Stacpoole, 88–91. London: Chapman, 1985.

———. *A New Pentecost?* New York: Seabury, 1975.

———. *Co-Responsibility in the Church*. New York: Herder, 1968.

———. *Memories and Hopes*. Dublin: Veritas, 1992.

Sullivan, Maureen. *The Road to Vatican II: Key Changes in Theology*. New York: Paulist Press, 2007.

Tanner, Kathryn. *Economy of Grace*. Minneapolis, MN: Fortress Press, 2005.

———. *Jesus, Humanity and the Trinity: A Brief Systematic Theology*. Minneapolis, MN: Fortress Press, 2001.

———. *The Politics of God: Christian Theologies and Social Justice*. Minneapolis, MN: Fortress Press, 1992.

Taylor, Charles. "Magisterial Authority." In *The Crisis of Authority in Catholic Modernity*, edited by Michael Lacey and Francis Oakley, 259–69. New York: Oxford University Press, 2011.

———. *A Secular Age*. Cambridge, MA: Belknap Press/Harvard University Press, 2007.

Theobald, Christoph. *"Dans les traces . . ." de la constitution "Dei Verbum" du concile Vatican II. Bible, théologie et pratiques de lecture*. Paris: Cerf, 2009.

———. "The Theological Options of Vatican II: Seeking an 'Internal' Principle of Interpretation." In *Concilium: Vatican II: A Forgotten Future*, edited by Alberto Melloni and Christoph Theobald, no. 4 (2005): 87–107.

———. *La réception du concile Vatican II: Accéder à la source*, vol. 1 Paris: Cerf, 2009.

Thiel, John. *Icons of Hope: The Last Things in Catholic Imagination*. Notre Dame, IN: University of Notre Dame Press, 2013.

Vance-Trembath, Sally. *The Pneumatology of Vatican II: With Particular Reference to* Lumen Gentium *and* Gaudium et Spes. Saarbrücken, Germany: Lambert Academic Publishing, 2009.

Villemin, Laurent. *Pouvoir d'ordre et pouvoir de juridiction: Histoire théologique de leur distinction*. Paris: Cerf, 2003.

Vorgrimler, Herbert, ed. *Commentary on the Documents of Vatican II*. 5 vols. New York: Crossroad, 1989.

Watson, Natalie. *Introducing Feminist Ecclesiology*. Eugene, OR: Wipf & Stock, 2008.

Weakland, Rembert G. *Pilgrim in a Pilgrim Church: Memoirs of a Catholic Archbishop*. Grand Rapids, MI: Eerdmans, 2009.

Wicks, Jared. "Vatican II on Revelation—From Behind the Scenes." *Theological Studies* 71 (2010): 637–50.

Wilde, Melissa J. *Vatican II: A Sociological Analysis of Religious Change*. Princeton, NJ: Princeton University Press, 2007.

Index

Ad Gentes, 65, 109–10
Affordable Care Act, 145–46
Aggiornamento ("up to date"), 35, 78
Ahern, Barnabus, 43
antepreparatory commission (Vatican II), 30–31
Aparecida document, 116
Apostolica Solicitudo, 64, 98
Apostolicam Actuositatem, 55, 77, 89, 103, 110
Apostolos Suos, 70, 97, 128
Aquinas, St. Thomas, 20, 22, 24, 74–75, 147
Aristotle, 20, 147
atheism, 85
Augustine of Hippo, St., 19–20, 23, 59, 74
authority, 87–89

Bacik, James, xvii, 142–43
Baldiserri, Cardinal Lorenzo, 124
baptism, 56, 57–60, 62, 87–99, 102–4, 106–7, 113, 136, 153
baptismal priesthood, 16, 58–59, 92, 112
Barron, Bishop Robert, 142, 143
Bea, Cardinal Augustine, 40
Beal, John, 104
Bellarmine, St. Robert, 11
Benedict XVI, Pope, xiv, 5, 7, 15, 46, 69, 97–98, 115–17, 127

biblical scholarship, 40, 51
bishops, 95–95, 97–99, 107–8
appointment of, 70, 94
College of Bishops, 95–96
episcopal collegiality, 63–65, 94–96
episcopal conferences, 15, 65, 97–98
episcopal ordinations, 98
Brooks, David, 148
Bugnini, Archbishop Annibale, xi

Cajetan, Cardinal Thomas, 11
Calvin, John, 20
canon law, x, 9, 30, 101, 104, 123, 126, 153
Cappellari, Mauro. *See* Gregory XVI
Carroll, Anthony, 142
Catechism of the Catholic Church, 15
Catholic Action, 102
Catholic identity, 25, 138–48
Catholic Worker Movement, 26
catholicity, 45, 147
CELAM, 116, 121, 133
charism, 60, 62, 102–4, 157
Christendom, 24
Christian Initiation, 58, 106–7
catechumenate, 106
Christian (Neo)-Platonism, 5, 10
Christocentrism, 50, 117, 142

Christus Dominus, x, 64–65, 77, 89, 95, 105

Church
  as pilgrim, 67–69, 79–81, 87–89, 150
  as sacrament, 61–62, 66, 77–78
  body of Christ, 16, 60, 67, 88, 93, 109, 150
  church/world relationship, 22–27, 35–36, 54, 57, 65–66, 86–87, 110
  office, 8–9, 46, 102–4
  people of God, 7, 55, 59, 68, 85, 88, 94, 100, 105, 107, 123, 129
  reform/renewal, xiii, xv, 81, 121, 137, 154–55, 157
  of Rome, 7–8, 63–64, 96, 97
  scandal, 144
  teaching, 36–37, 51, 133–34, 143–45, 149
  temple of the Holy Spirit, 61, 150

Cicognani, Cardinal Amleto, 34, 39
clericalism, 70
Clifford, Catherine, xvii, 45, 130
Coetus Internationalis Patrum, 41
College of Cardinals, 2, 11, 125
conciliar commissions (Vatican II), 38–39
conciliarism, 11, 93
confirmation, 59, 106
Congar, Yves, 4, 9, 11, 33, 42, 60–61, 93, 102, 118–19, 145
Congregation for Divine Worship, xi, 140
Congregation for the Discipline of the Sacraments, xi, 140
Congregation for the Doctrine of the Faith, 31, 46, 129
Consilium, x

Constantinian Settlement, 23
consultation of the faithful, 86, 100–101, 123–26
consumerism, 139, 142, 149
conversion, 137
council of cardinals, 125
Council of Constance, 10
Council of Florence, 10–11
Council of Trent, 6, 11, 21, 136
Cullman, Oscar, 53
curia, x, 11, 14, 30–31, 34–35, 44–45, 98, 129
Cyprian of Carthage, St. 46, 62

Day, Dorothy, 26
Dei Verbum, 49–53, 66, 82–84, 99–100
development of doctrine, 2, 36–37, 52, 64, 134
dialogue, 14, 37, 45, 53–57, 79, 85–87, 110, 122–26, 147
Dignitatis Humanae, 68
divinization, 19
doctrine, 36–38, 52, 84–85, 129–35, 140–41, 143, 144–45
  reception of, 7, 87
dogma, 6, 13, 52–53
Dolan, Jay, 26
Dominus Iesus, 69
Domus Mariae, 40–41
Döpfner, Cardinal Julius, 29, 33–34
Duffy, Eamon, 21, 135

Eastern Catholic Churches, 33, 43, 64
ecclesial learning, 46, 51, 98–101
Ecclesiam Suam, 54, 85
ecumenism/ecumenical dialogue, 38, 53–54, 56, 77, 79, 81, 86, 97–98, 139–40

Enlightenment, 3, 24, 110
eschatology, 67–68
Eucharist, 16, 21, 94–95, 104–8, 131, 154–55
Evangelii Gaudium, 116–18, 121–23, 128, 130–31

Faggioli, Massimo, 44, 79, 104
Federation of Asian Bishops Conferences, 127
First Vatican Council, 12–13, 63–64, 95
Foucault, Michel, 153–54
Francis, Pope, xvi, 45, 47, 98, 101, 115–36, 142, 147, 150–52, 155
Franco-Prussian War, 13
Fransen, Piet, 43
French Revolution, 3, 12, 24
Frings, Cardinal Josef, 29, 39–40
Fullam, Lisa, 74–75

Gaudet Mater Ecclesia, 35
Gaudium et Spes, 51–52, 54, 57, 65–66, 85, 100, 110
grace, 18–22, 67–68, 91–92
Gregorian reforms, 8–10
Gregory VII, St. Pope, 8–10
Gregory XVI, Pope, 12, 25

Haec Sancta, 10
Hahnenberg, Edward, 156
Hamer, Cardinal Jean Jérôme, 127
Hellemans, Staf, 3, 139
Henn, William, 9
hermeneutic of discontinuity, xiv
hermeneutic of reform, xiv
hierarchy, 105, 120
hierarchy of truths, xii, 53, 84, 129–30
historical consciousness, 37, 52, 81, 144

Holy Office. *See* Congregation for the Doctrine of the Faith
Holy Spirit, xvi, 2, 22, 50–51, 60–63, 83, 87, 91–100, 102–4, 106, 109–10, 113, 122, 130, 153, 156, 158
Humanae Vitae, 132–33
Humani Generis, 13
humility, xvi, 73–89, 117, 138–41, 144–48, 151–52
Hunter, James Davison, 154

inculturation, 15
Industrial Revolution, 24–25
International Theological Commission (ITC), 46–47, 119, 123
interreligious dialogue, 57, 86
intraecclesial dialogue, 85–86
Ivereigh, Austen, 115

Jean Eudes, St., 17
Jesus Christ, 5, 7, 50, 58, 83, 106, 117, 129–30, 142, 153, 158
John XXIII, St. Pope, xv, 13, 25, 29, 33–34, 35, 39–40, 43, 54, 61, 78–79, 133, 136, 151
John of Torquemada, Cardinal, 11
John Paul II, St. Pope, 14–15, 69–70, 97–98, 100, 115–16, 127–28, 130, 141, 145

Kasper, Walter, xv
Keenan, James, 75–76, 87
kerygma, 129–31
koinonia, 97
Komonchak, Joseph, xvi, 31, 94, 127
Küng, Hans, 44

Lafont, Ghislain, 4–5, 15, 106

laity, xi, 111–12
  lay ministry, 62
  relationship with clergy, 15–18,
    55–56, 70, 102, 108–9,
    111–12
Lakeland, Paul, 73
Langan, John, 134
Lash, Nicholas, 141
Lefebvre, Cardinal Marcel, 41
Léger, Cardinal Paul-Émile, 29, 34,
  40
Legrand, Hervé, x
Leo XIII, Pope, 25
Lercaro, Cardinal Giacomo, x–xi
Liénart, Cardinal Achille, 29, 34,
  39–40
liturgy, x–xi, 2, 21, 43, 58, 65–66,
  70, 79–80, 94–95, 104–9, 126
  liturgical reform/renewal, x–xi,
    80
local church, 9, 12, 17, 97, 107,
  127–28
  relationship to universal church,
    94–95
Lonergan, Bernard, 144
Luciani, Bishop Albino (Pope
  John Paul I), 43
Lumen Gentium, 55, 58–59,
  61–63, 64, 66, 67–68, 77–78,
  80, 83, 87–88, 95–96, 100, 103,
  111
Luther, Martin, 20, 58
Lyon, David, 138–39

magisterium, 6–7, 13, 37, 50–52,
  82, 98–101, 126, 128, 145
Magnani, Giovanni, 111
magnanimity, 75, 78, 81, 138,
  141–44, 152
Malone, Matt, 146
Mannion, Gerard, 73

Marmion, Columba, 18
Maximos IV Saigh, Patriarch, 33
mercy, 37, 116–18, 131
Miller, Vincent, 139, 141, 147
ministerial priesthood, 2, 16, 57,
  88, 108, 128, 156
  sacral priesthood, 15–18
ministry, 156–57
mission, xiv, 55, 57, 65–66, 77,
  82, 104, 109, 110–11, 116–22,
  152–53
missionary discipleship, 116, 119,
  152
modernism, 24–25
monasticism, 24
Montini, Cardinal Giovanni. *See*
  Paul VI, Pope
moral discernment, 134
Mortalium Animos, 38
Murray, John Courtney, 26
Mystici Corporis, 93

Napoleon III, 12
neoscholasticism, 6, 98–99
neotriumphalism, 140
new evangelization, 116
Newman, John Henry, 13, 63
Nostra Aetate, 56–57, 86
nota praevia, 14, 64, 96, 105

O'Brien, John, 37–38
O'Donovan, Leo, 143
O'Loughlin, John, 42
O'Malley, John, xvi, 8, 54, 76
Optatam Totius, 52–53
order, 106–7
ordination, 88, 97–98, 107,
  156–57
Ordo Concilii, 32
Origen, 23
Osborne, Kenan B., 112

Ottaviani, Cardinal Alfredo, 35,
40, 43

papacy, 1, 7–15, 95–96
Bishop of Rome, 64
monarchial, 12
papal authority, 14, 93–94
papal centralization, 3
papal encyclicals, 13
papal infallibility, 13, 63
papal supremacy, 64
papal teaching authority, 135
relationship to bishops, 94–98
Paschal Mystery, 62
Pastor Aeternus, 12–13
Pastores Gregis, 127
Paul, St., 8
Paul VI, Pope, 12–14, 33–34, 39, 46,
54, 64, 85, 98, 115, 132–33, 145
Paulinus of Nola, St., 100
Pentecost, 61
Perfectae Caritatis, 77
periti, 32, 42
Peter, St., 8
Phillippe, Paul, 31
Pierre de Bérulle, 17
Pius IX, Pope, 12, 25
Pius X, Pope, 25, 57, 98
Pius XI, Pope, 38, 102
Pius XII, Pope, 13, 14, 60, 93
pneumatology, xvi, 60–63, 91, 93,
122
Pontifical Council for Peace and
Justice, 14
Pottmeyer, Hermann, xiii–xiv, 4, 69
power, 75–76, 87–89, 104, 117,
153–57
preparatory commissions (Vatican
II), 30–31
presbyterate. *See* ministerial
priesthood

Presbyterorum Ordinis, 56, 88–89,
77, 103
prophecy, 120
Protestant Reformation, xi, 3, 11,
20–22, 24, 58
Pseudo-Dionysius, 5, 10

Rahner, Karl, 33, 43
Ratzinger, Cardinal Joseph. *See*
Benedict XVI, Pope
reconciliation, 152–53, 155–56
religious life, 55, 120
ressourcement, 106, 128
revelation, 39–40, 50, 51, 53, 83–
84, 87, 98–99, 129–30, 143
Routhier, Gilles, xii, 29
Ruffini, Cardinal Ernesto, 40
Rule of Benedict, 155
Ryan, John A., 26

sacraments, 18–22
Sacrosanctum Concilium, 58, 65,
67, 79–80, 94–96, 104–6, 126
salvation, 7, 67, 92, 143
Schillebeeckx, Edward, 32, 33,
111–12
Schotte, Cardinal Jan, 127
Schüssler Fiorenza, Elizabeth, 2–3,
105
Scientific Revolution, 24
Scripture, interpretation of, 6
Secretariat of State, Vatican, 14
secularism, 69, 117, 138–40
Segundo, Juan Luis, 140
selection of bishops, 9
sensus fidei, xi, 52, 62–63, 82,
99–101, 118, 122–23
infallibility of, 122
sensus fidelium, 123
simony, 8
sin, 18–19, 67, 80

Sixtus V, Pope 11
Smith, James K. A., 154
subsidiarity, 126–29
Suenens, Cardinal Leó-Joseph, 29,
   31, 33–34, 39–40, 60, 61
synod of bishops, 64, 70, 97–98,
   126, 132
   1985 Extraordinary Synod of
    Bishops (1985), 127
   2014 Synod of Bishops, 124–25
synodality, 124

Tardini, Cardinal Domenico, 30–31
Taylor, Charles, 138, 145
Tedeschi, Bishop Giacomo Radini,
   44
Theobald, Christoph, 37, 50
theologian, 119–20, 123
Tisserant, Cardinal Eugéne, 39
tradition, 51–52, 100, 148–49
Trinity, 49–53, 62, 82–83, 96, 99,
   106, 109

triumphalism, 67, 69, 81, 82,
   139–40, 141, 144
Tromp, Sebastian, 31

Ultramontanism, 3, 12
Unitatis Redintegratio, 53, 56, 78,
   81, 129
Ut Unum Sint, 97, 130

Vincent de Paul, St., 17
virtue, 73–76
virtue ethics, 75–76

Weakland, Archbishop Rembert, 14
Wilde, Melissa, 40–41
Word of God, 40, 51, 62–63, 82,
   99, 119–20, 123
World War II, 26
Wright, Cardinal John, 112

Zizola, Giancarlo, 43
Zwingli, Ulrich, 21